HEALING THE HEART

HEALING THE HEART

Getting to the Root of Abuse, PTSD and Trauma

Rev. Millie McCarty, M.A., LPCC SUPR

Charleston, SC
www.PalmettoPublishing.com

Healing the Heart: Getting to the Root of Abuse, PTSD and Trauma

Copyright © 2022 by Rev. Millie McCarty, M.A., LPCC

Faith-based trauma training developed in 2013 for International Missions

Taught in China, Ethiopia, Rwanda, Jamaica, Uganda, Finland, Haiti and Cuba

Copyright ©2002

Revised for publication 2020

All rights reserved

No portion of this book may be reproduced, stored in a retrieval system, or transmitted in any form by any means–electronic, mechanical, photocopy, recording, or other–except for brief quotations in printed reviews, without prior permission of the author.

Requests for information should be addressed to:

The Healing Hub at the Gate
Pickerington, Ohio 43147

milliehealinghub4u@gmail.com

First Edition

Paperback ISBN: 978-1-7354796-0-6

eBook ISBN: 979-8-8229-1727-9

DEDICATION

I dedicate this book to those who poured into my spirit the Truth of God's Word, but also opened doors of opportunity to learn and serve in and through the church. I had the best of pastors, sat under the teaching of some of the best authors, practitioners, psychologists, counselors, and others who asked the same questions "What happened?" and "What can be done?" As I searched for answers to the unknown realm of trauma, it was those who had gone before me who provided the books, articles, workshops, and research that led to the steps that guided my daily search for answers. This book is the compilation of knowledge from years of reading, taking classes, going to workshops, and counseling some of the most deeply wounded people, now for 40 years of counseling, which led to my writing and teaching others who work with trauma survivors.

The true pioneers were those whom I have quoted in this book and used their materials and knowledge to bring healing to thousands of people in nations I had never dreamed of visiting. It has been my privilege and blessing to practice and then to provide training in places like China and Rwanda where there had been extreme persecution and trauma…learning as I taught the effectiveness of the curriculum in setting people free and laying a groundwork for re-building their lives. I have been blessed beyond my wildest imagination to be used of God in this way. I pray you will be blessed as you partake of the wisdom and knowledge, I share with you and pray you will have the blessing of being a part of God's army of healers.

Last, but not least, I dedicate this book to the hundreds of deeply wounded survivors who were courageous enough to step up and tell their stories and endure the psychological pain of remembering and working through the lies and faulty perceptions they believed as a result of the unbelievably cruel things done to children. Each one deserves an award, for to me they are the heroes in the cause of redeeming the lives of the lost and wounded. What I learned from them helped me understand what others were experiencing, and ultimately was able to use internationally as I have taken this curriculum to thousands in other countries.

Millie McCarty, M.A., LPCC-S

Graduating *Cum Laude* from Defiance College with a B. A. Degree in Religious Education, Millie went on to receive her M.A. degree in Guidance and Counseling from The Ohio State University in 1981 and became a Licensed Professional Clinical Counselor in 1985. Millie's background as a Director of Education at her church and a Parenting Educator as well as a Personal Growth & Development Trainer added to the richness of her knowledge and ability to meet people where their need was.

Widely known in Ohio as a counselor and teacher, Millie served 20 years as the founder and Executive Director of *Lighthouse Counseling Services from 1981–2001,* when she retired to write and teach. Her groundbreaking work in the areas of early childhood sexual, ritual abuse and Dissociative Identity Disorder, has brought healing and restoration through her strategic, systematic design combining faith principles and proven professional strategies to thousands of adult victims of childhood sexual trauma to citizens of Ohio

After retiring, Millie began a ten-year journey of co-writing a case study entitled *RUTH: Secret of the Silenced voices (A Guide to Working with People with Dissociative Identity Disorders)*. During this period from 2002–2012, as a by-product of the case study, Millie wrote her next book *WHY WE CAN'T "Just Get Over It": Healing the Effects of Prolonged Stress and Trauma.* At the same time, developing her *"Systematic Process"* of resolving unresolved conflicts needed for restoration. Millie began being asked to train people from other nations such as: China, Ethiopia, Jamaica, Finland, Haiti, Rwanda and Uganda. Today she is being called to train church leaders at home and abroad in her Systematic Process to equip the church for the great harvest that lies before us.

Systematic Process for Resolving Unresolved Conflict Eternally (SPRUCE)

From 2012–2017 Millie implemented a systematic approach to equipping others with the tools to provide care for survivors of abuse and trauma using her curriculum and implementing other coursework to provide the necessary skills to restore the life skills missed during the time of abuse and trauma. These classes were established as a certification program based on her 35 years of counseling and training. Her ultimate goal is to get the curriculum accredited and published to provide this **S**ystematic **P**rocess of **R**esolving **U**nresolved **C**onflict **E**ternally (**SPRUCE**) to all nations.

This Healing the Heart was originally **TRAUMA RECOVERY TRAINING—a** course designed specifically to take to the nations. It contains excerpts from PATHWAYS TO HOPE AND HEALING, Copyright©2002 and WHY WE CAN'T "JUST GET OVER IT", Copyright ©2009, both written by Millie McCarty, M.A., LPCC. All rights reserved. No part of this publication may be reproduced, transmitted in any form or stored in a retrieval system without prior written permission of author, except in the case of brief quotations embodied in articles and previews.

CONTENT AND GOALS:

Healing the Heart (formerly Trauma Recovery Training) is a composite of both books developed by founder, Millie McCarty, MA., LPCC-Supervisor; <u>Pathways to Hope and Healing</u> and <u>Why We Can't "Just Get Over It".</u> In order to bring the core teachings of healing ministry, we have chosen the most important sections of these two books in order to accomplish the following goals:

- To train participants in Millie's systematic approach to healing survivors of abuse and trauma using her unique **SPRUCE** process:

> **Systematic Process for Resolving Unresolved Conflict Eternally (SPRUCE)**

- To help participants apply the Biblical principles of healing to their own trauma-based thoughts, emotions and actions.
- To begin to understand the amazing neurological connection between the brain and gut and the power of our thoughts over our body's system that is designed to protect us; and how to begin to direct that energy and power in such a way that it brings healing instead of disease.
- To train participants in the systematic use of eight assessment tools that assist in getting to the root issues beneath the surface of the mental, emotional and behavioral root causes of stress and trauma. Once the roots have been uncovered, we learn how to do "Spiritual Surgery" to literally "take the ax to the root" ... rooting out the lies and replacing them with God's truth.... thus, facilitating their healing from trauma.

<u>Why We Can't "Just Get Over It"</u> was written as a result of a ten-year assignment to write a Case Study **<u>RUTH: Secrets of the Silenced Voices</u>**; the story of the life of one lady who had experienced a lifetime of abuse and trauma at the hands of her family and live-in friend of the father who was a pedophile. Her life included every kind of abuse and torture including Satanic Ritual Abuse, yet she went on to be functional as a schoolteacher and executive employee in the State Dept. of Social Services as well as maintaining a strong belief in God. Ruth lived to tell her story and to assist Millie in teaching the first class of RUTH as well as teaching <u>Why We Can't "Just Get Over It"</u> in China two times and Ethiopia before going home to her eternal peace in 2017.

TABLE OF CONTENTS

SESSION 1—INTRODUCTION TO HEALING THE HEART 1
    Effects of Disasters vs. Effects of Abuse.. 1
    Stress: Good, Bad and Overload 3
    Trauma: Definition 4
    Thoughts Determine Our Destiny 5
    How Thoughts Develop 6
    Limbic System... 7
    The 'Stress Ball' Theory... 7
    Inhibitory Pathway 9
    Information Molecules... 10
    The Heart's Brain.. 11
    Molecules of Emotion—The Crucial Link 11
    Updated Statistics 12
    System Damage Due to Stress and Trauma 15

SESSION TWO—THE POWER OF THE MIND 16
    Faith and Fear... 16
    Post-Traumatic Stress Disorder 16
    Childhood Trauma.. 17
    Developmental Problems 19
    Arrested Development.. 23
    Abnormal Coping Behaviors 23
    Unresolved Conflict.. 24
    Cyclical Thinking 24
    Social or Relational Issues 26

SESSION THREE—DEALING WITH ANGRY PEOPLE 28
    Six Ways to Deal with Angry People... 28
    Cognitive Distortions 29
    The Mind: A Battleground between Good and Evil.. 30
    Four Rules for Controlling Your Thought Life 31
    Flashbacks and Triggers 32
    Nervous System—Main Target of Toxic Thoughts... 34

SESSION FOUR—TREE OF BONDAGE VS. TREE OF FREEDOM 37
    From Darkness Into His Light 39
    Cycle of Dysfunction 41
    Cycle of Illumination—Five Steps of Shedding the Light 45
    Cycle of Illumination—Activity—Shedding the Light 45

SESSION FIVE—FROM DARKNESS TO LIGHT ... 48
- Jo-Hari Window ... 48
- Generational Sins ... 50
- The Ten Commandments ... 51
- Blessings and Curses ... 52
- The Genogram ... 54
- Looking for Root Causes of Problems ... 54
- Reflective Exercise ... 58

SESSION SIX—EQUIPPING GOD'S PEOPLE ... 60
- Our Brother's Keeper ... 60
- Principalities Over Families and Nations ... 60
- Days of Ezekiel ... 62
- Equipping for Warfare—Holy Spirit ... 63
- Know God's Word ... 66
- Armor of God ... 67

SESSION SEVEN—WEB OF LIES ... 72
- Sowing and Reaping ... 72
- Types of Lies We Believe ... 73
- Memories Hold Lies ... 74
- Defense Mechanisms ... 76
- Personal Reflective Exercise ... 79
- Cycle of Dysfunction ... 80

SESSION EIGHT—THE FAMILY SYSTEMS MODEL ... 84
- Rules, Roles, Rituals, Standards, Beliefs and Values ... 85
- Family Makes A Difference—Four Basic Family Types ... 89
- God's Perception vs. My Perception ... 91

SESSION NINE—BREAKING FREE ... 92
- Guide to Spiritual Surgery ... 92
- Repentance ... 94
- Inner Vows & Oaths ... 96
- Forgiveness ... 97
- Cycle of Illumination ... 100
- Dying to Self ... 100
- Books Written by Millie McCarty, M.A., LPCC ... 103
- Bibliography ... 105
- Reference Notes ... 114

Session One

INTRODUCTION TO HEALING THE HEART

Introduction

➢ Why do we do the things we don't want to do, but *don't* do the things we *want* to do?
➢ Why is it that no matter how much we know, we keep going back to our old thinking and old ways of doing things?
➢ Why is change so difficult? Why is it so difficult to 'put the past behind us?'

Effects of Disasters vs. Effects of Abuse

Disasters and abuse, especially sexual abuse, have different effects on victims. One significant difference between sexual abuse and victims of other types of abuse and disasters is that there is so much shame and guilt connected to sexual abuse. When a child is sexually violated, they have no way of defending themselves and most have no understanding of what is happening, therefore they have no way of telling. The major differences are:

Effects of Disasters: victims...
- Draw attention from media
- Are provided with social service assistance
- Elicit sympathy and help from the community, forming a type of support system
- Receive short-term, if not long-term meeting of needs

Effects of Abuse: victims...
- Rarely get acknowledged and in most cases are not validated, rather, accused, and their cries are not heard
- Are held in suspicion and shame and are expected to get over it without help or support of any kind
- Keep 'the secret' because of further threat of retaliation
- Withdraw and keep quiet out of guilt and shame and to avoid public reaction of disgust and distrust

As a result, they often come to embrace the belief that they are to blame, without knowing what they did to cause it. This only increases the shame and guilt, as well as the pain. They often hide behind walls of fear, intimidation, anger, bitterness, revenge, and resentful unforgiveness. They waste away.
   Most victims of abuse do not seek help on their own for the original injury. Instead:

- It usually takes a major outburst or eruption—one that draws the attention of the police, school officials, or medical or mental health agencies—to get them help

- Lack of training in trauma and abuse for agency workers often results in little real help, so, blame continues.
- The necessity to discover the deeper secret is not considered or addressed due to the urgency of the immediate problem. The prevailing belief is that the past should just be forgotten, and life should go on as usual.

Most have waited to come for help until their 30's, 40's, or 50's—some are even older. These are people who held their trauma as a secret within them until their lives became dysfunctional, causing problems in their marriages, families, jobs or health. Most have made the rounds to doctors and psychiatrists, have been in and out of hospitals—often times being told by doctors that there was nothing physically wrong.

Many had recurring panic attacks, mood disorders, anxiety disorders, and dissociative identity disorder (DID)—many with Post Traumatic Stress Disorder (PTSD) and anger issues as well. Some have bodies that simply wore out from carrying their trauma as prisoner.

We will learn that when trauma strikes—no matter the age or gender—it has a dramatic effect on the life of the survivor. They become anxious, angry, bitter and negative. They are susceptible to thought distortions which lead to physical and mental problems. Without help, they develop behavioral, mental or relational addictions. Trauma changes lives. If you have experienced any type of trauma, you will be helped in your understanding of what has happened (and may still be happening) to you by completing this course.

> *When I Kept Silent, My Bones Waxed old Through My Roaring All Day Long. For Day and Night thy Hand was Heavy Upon Me; My moisture is Turned into the Drought of Summer. I Acknowledged my Sin to You, and Mine Iniquity I have not Hid. I said, 'I Will Confess My Transgressions to the Lord,' and thou Forgavest the Iniquity of My Sin. —Psalm 32:3-5*

We are going to be examining lifestyles, mindsets and behaviors considering stress and trauma. It is important that we understand what people experience during traumatic events. We will recognize the control that fear, pride and self-deception can have over their lives.

> *You will Learn About Cultural Changes Which Sadly Have Brought About Generations of Child Sexual, Mental, and Emotional Abuse of Our Children*

You will meet a survivor, a child in an adult body, who embodies the trauma experiences of millions of children in our world today. She is symbolic of the attack on children. She has chosen to tell her story to let the world know that in a fallen world, sin steals the childhoods of our sons and daughters, uses them, abuses them, neglects them, turns them into little adults—anything to steal or block God's purpose for their lives.

What Keeps Them in Bondage?
- Lack of Knowledge
- Believing this kind of life is 'normal'
- Secrets Used by the Enemy to Deceive
- Unwillingness to Forgive

Stress Definition: Stress is pressure, strain, a force that tends to distort a body—a factor that induces bodily or mental tension. Stress is the body's way of rising to a challenge and preparing to meet a tough situation with focus, strength, stamina, and heightened alertness.

Physicist, Hans Selye, says stress differs for everyone. He used a roller coaster ride as an example: some people are petrified, and others are thrilled to get on and ride. All experimental and clinical research confirms that the sense of having little or no control is always stressful—and that's what stress is all about.

Stress—whether it be good stress or bad stress—can still have an impact on us. Good Stress might include things like:
- A new job
- Marriage
- Getting a new home
- A new baby

Challenging tasks may keep you on your toes, ready to rise to the challenge, but one can return to a normal state quickly.

Bad Stress includes such things as:
- Coping with divorce
- Moving to a new neighborhood or school
- Long-term illness of a loved one
- Loss of a job

Stress Overload
This occurs when any of the above pressures are too intense, last too long, or are shouldered alone, such as:
- Domestic violence
- Constant family conflicts
- Multiple losses
- Ongoing financial, work, health or family problems without support
- Living with person(s) with addictions

- **Signs of Stress Overload**
  - Anxiety or panic attacks
  - A feeling of being constantly pressured, hassled, and hurried
  - Explosive anger in response to minor irritations
  - Irritability and moodiness
  - Physical symptoms like fatigue, stomach problems, headaches or chest pain
  - Sleep disturbances
  - Menstrual distress
  - Loss of appetite
  - Ulcers
  - Intestinal problems
  - Heart palpitations
  - Lower back pain
  - Allergy or asthma attacks
  - Drinking too much, smoking, overeating, or doing drugs

Keeping Stress Under Control
- Avoid over-scheduling
- Be realistic in your expectations
- Get a good night's sleep
- Build time in your schedule to relax
- Treat your body well (exercise, eat well)
- Watch what you are thinking
- Solve the little problems that can pile up
- Think of change as a challenging, normal part of life, and think of problems as temporary and solvable
- Believe that you will succeed if you keep working toward your goals
- Build strong relationships and keep commitments
- Have a support system and ask for help
- Relax, laugh and have fun

> *I will Walk Among You and Be Your God, and Ye shall Be My People.* —Leviticus 26:12

TRAUMA: Definition
Trauma is an emotional shock that creates significant and lasting damage to a person's mental, physical, and emotional growth. It can also be caused by interpersonal violence over the life span, including sexual abuse, physical abuse, severe neglect, loss, or witnessing violence. (National Association of State Mental Health Program Directors)

The Human Body is an amazing instrument:
- It houses a brain that has one trillion synaptic connections
- It gives us ten million new cells every second
- There are 3.2 billion cells in a DNA cell
- Our brain is organized to record our environment which causes us to think

Our environment provides us opportunity to gain knowledge and experience.
If we don't change the environment, we don't grow.
- At six months in the womb, a fetus begins to develop neurons which begin making connections as soon as knowledge enters
- The embryo will have specific traits of the parents—especially those they practice most (50% of who we are comes from our parents, 50% from our environment)
- We make our own chemical connections from 1) Knowledge, and 2) Experience

Believe It or Not, there *is* a Greater Intelligence
Dr. Joe Dispenza states in *Rewiring Your Brain to a New Reality,* that, "there is a greater intelligence living within us that gives us life."
- His <u>Mind</u> is much <u>Greater</u> than ours
- His <u>Will</u> is <u>Stronger</u> than ours
- His <u>Love</u> is <u>More</u> than ours
- He <u>Gives Life</u> and <u>Order</u> to the universe
- He <u>Keeps</u> the <u>Heart Beating</u> and gives life
- He <u>Provides Digestion</u> and the <u>Ability to Breathe</u>
- He <u>Designed</u> our <u>Brain</u> to have the ability to redistribute chemicals in order to "<u>heal itself</u>".

> *Our Thoughts, Emotions and Will Can Interfere With His Love and Care for Us*

Thoughts Determine Our Destiny
- To change is to think and act greater than our environment.
- We must embrace our destiny and live it even if our environment isn't in agreement. This is a sign of greatness.
- Our thoughts create a new template for the brain.
- As we meditate on the new experience, we tell the mind what we want, and the body recreates it.
- As we repeat the same thought over and over, we force the brain to think, and it responds by firing new neurons, reconditioning the body to agree with the mind.

There Are Three Brains
- One in the Head,
  - One in the Heart, and,
    - One in the Gastrointestinal Tract.

The brain in the GI Tract is in the lining of the esophagus, stomach, small intestine and colon. The brain and the gut (or digestive tract) are connected. The GI tract and the brain come from the same part of the developing baby, or embryo. As a result, the digestive tract and brain form a complex circuit with nerve cells (neurons), and chemicals that relay signals (neurotransmitters) that relay signals and messages, and proteins (neuropeptides) that enable the brain and gut to act independently and interdependently; to remember, learn and produce "gut feelings."

Research shows that in your Heart you have a little mini brain of 40,000 neurons, or, nerve cells, and that the little heart's brain is a *checking station*.
- It checks for accuracy, for truth and for congruence
- It is a small quiet voice, the conscience. On a spiritual level, it would be where the Holy Spirit would speak to you
- As thoughts pass through your conscience, they are formed
- Your thoughts create a state of being

How Thoughts Develop
It is important to understand how thoughts develop, how the thoughts grow in your brain, and how memories are stored because your thoughts and memories ultimately affect your health negatively or positively. Dr. Caroline Leaf (*Who Switched Off My Brain* ©2009(1)) states that:

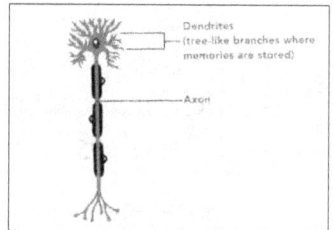

- Thoughts are like a tree with a trunk and many branches; the more branches, the more intelligent and accessible the thoughts will be.
- Each thought is made up of cells called neurons.
- At the end of each neuron are branches called dendrites—highly complex structures involved in the process of receiving and integrating information coming in via the five senses.
- The information is translated into electrical impulses and transported across synapses (small chemical gaps) between neurons that form interconnected neural circuits. There are volumes written on the function of dendrites. I suggest if you are interested, get on the internet and Google "dendrites" and enjoy.

When thoughts are pushed aside or considered unnecessary, dendrites droop and break. Glial cells, that provide support and resources such as nourishment, protection, and cleaning, work while we sleep to eliminate weak and broken dendrites and care for connections. When we control, process and integrate thoughts, we provide healthy environments.

Limbic System

The _limbic system_ gives thought the emotional and physiological part of your life. It is the emotional center of your mind and made up of the _hippocampus_, the _amygdala_ and _hypothalamus._ These are interconnected and play a role in creating a biochemical representation of a thought by:
- processing that thought,
- building memory, and,
- giving thought the emotional and physiological part of your life.

It is the _limbic system_ which connects the mind and body. Everything that concerns thoughts—both good and bad—travels up and down this connective pathway. The _limbic lobe, hippocampus, amygdala_ and _thalamus_ also play vital roles in explaining what a thought is, how it grows and how it produces emotions and physiological responses in your mind.

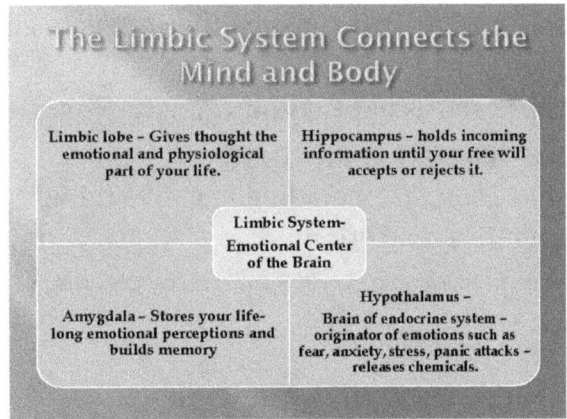

Remember also, that your heart has a mini brain that operates like a checking station that evaluates the wisdom of thoughts, keeping rash decisions and impulsive thinking under control.

> _Out of the Abundance of the Heart, the Mouth Speaketh._ —Matt. 12:34

THE 'STRESS BALL' THEORY

The brain is connected to the emotions. There are many factors that contribute to forming this ball of stress. It is easy to demonstrate by the following diagram, except multiplied many times over. People can go through this cycle when: a bill comes that they can't afford to pay, when an unexpected guest comes to visit, when the boss says, "come to my office," or, when a deadline for a project arrives and it is nowhere near being done. The cycle goes like this: (1) <u>Perceived Stress</u> leads to a (2) <u>Fight-or-Flight Response,</u> which (3) <u>Opens the 'Gate' to Symptoms</u> and the descending inhibitory pathway for pain control and to the rest of the bio-chemical system in your body. As a result, pain threshold is lowered with an increased sensitivity to pain and symptoms. Therefore, (4) the <u>Gastrointestinal and Bodily Symptoms</u> or somatization (physical problems) occur. People vary in their ability to recognize and distinguish whether their bodily symptoms are coming from a physical problem, or, from stress, emotions, or psychological problems. (Taken from *Irritable Bowel Syndrome* by Dr. William B. Salt II (1)

Other Things that Add to the Cycle of Stress
- *Poor Social Support* from family, friends and co-workers.
- *Lack of Faith and Spirituality.* There is increasing evidence of the value of faith and spirituality in stress management and healing.
- *Poor Self-Care and General Health Habits* like a healthy diet, exercise, rest, and relaxation.
- *A History of Abuse.* Studies now clearly show that a history of physical, emotional or sexual abuse in the early developmental years can lead to a form of post-traumatic stress disorder which either causes or magnifies the pain and symptoms, both physical and emotional.
- *Nature/Nurture Issues* such as susceptibility to somatization. These are probably related to factors that are both genetic and inherited (nature) as well as environmental (nurture).
- *Triggers or Perceptions of Past Pain* that can then activate gut symptoms and some other bodily symptoms.
- *Psychological Problems* such as depression, anxiety, panic disorder, and history of abuse which can then lead to negative emotions and thoughts.
- *Negative Emotions and Thoughts* including negative thinking, irrational and distorted beliefs and thoughts, and cognitive distortions.

(Taken from *Irritable Bowel Syndrome* by Dr. William B. Salt II. (2))

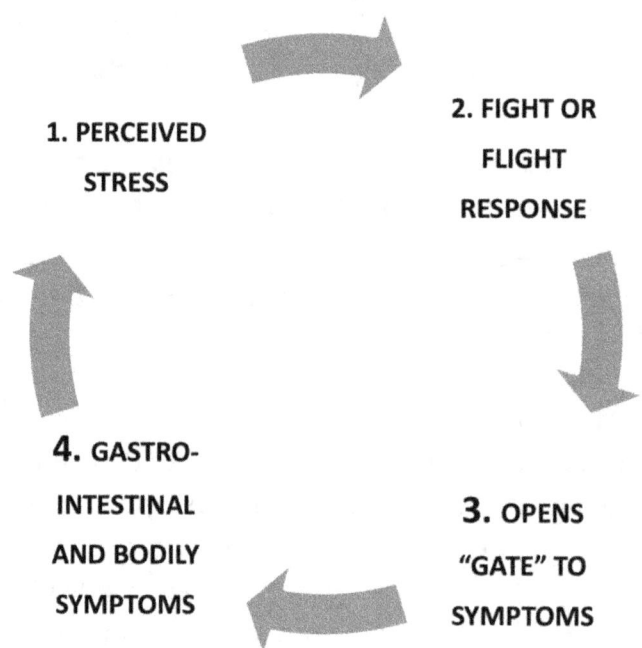

Bio-Chemical Pathway
How the brain can modify the feeling of pain and symptoms:

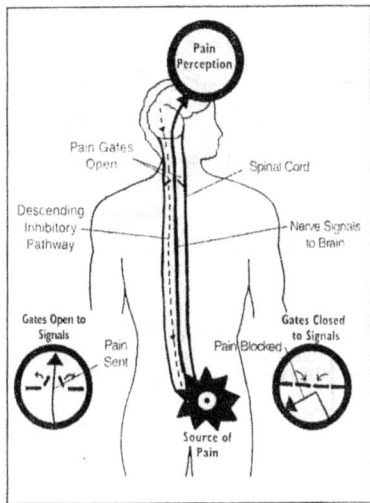

The brain is the control center of the body. Think of a telephone operator who answers incoming calls and directs them to where they need to go. Similarly, your brain acts as an operator by sending messages from all over the body to their proper destination. Since the brain is one of the largest and most important organs of the human body (weighing in at about three pounds); this organ has a wide range of responsibilities—from coordinating our movement to managing our emotions.

Inhibitory Pathway
Symptoms coming from the body and GI tract to the brain through the spinal cord can be either enhanced and worsened or blocked and reduced through the 'inhibitory pathway'. *(Irritable Bowel Syndrome;* Dr. William B. Salt, II.) The diagram above shows pathways coming from the brain down to the spinal cord. Stimulation of these descending pathways can reduce and even abolish some forms of pain. The body also produces chemicals including *opioids* that act on the same receptors to provide pain relief. The significance of descending inhibitory pathways and chemicals is the control and modification of pain sensations.

In recent decades, the advent of brain-imaging technology, such as the MRI, has allowed scientists and researchers to watch how the part of the brain called the *amygdala* as it responds to danger. One study found that:
- The *amygdala* becomes active even when subjects are shown photographs of faces that appear to be frightening.
- Various chemicals, including stress hormones and adrenalin, are released when the *amygdala* perceives a threat.

"We actually build double memories of everything," says Dr. Caroline Leaf, PhD., author of *Who Switched off My Brain* (Switch on Your Brain USA, Inc., publisher, 2008) (2). She points out that:
- The left brain works from detail to the big picture.
- The right brain works from the big picture to detail.

- The two sides work in synergy to process every thought.
- The more processing the brain does, the *more* and the *healthier* the memories.
- The information we think about comes in from five senses: sight, hearing, touch, smell and taste.
- Memory is built on <u>neurons</u> (nerve cells) and exists in neuron branches called <u>dendrites</u>. There are *100 trillion neurons,* and each can grow *70,000 dendrites* of memory storage. As mentioned earlier, when thoughts are pushed aside or considered unnecessary, dendrites droop and break.
- The human brain can store *300 million years* of memory.

Information Molecules (carriers of emotion)
- The brain secretes chemicals according to the emotions your thoughts generate.
- These chemicals have an electromagnetic charge that carries a photocopy of memories developed and sorted within the mind.
- They travel around your body affecting and influencing the various systems in an ordered sequence.
- Cells constantly signal other cells through the release of brain chemicals known as <u>neuropeptides</u> which bind with receptors.
- Any cellular changes from an excess of stress hormones corrode or change the shape of the receptors which allows foreign <u>neurochemicals</u> or viruses to get into the cell.
- Cells signal other cells and they feed back into peptide-secreting cells, telling them how much more or less to secrete.
- Toxic thoughts disrupt the flow of feedback loops, interrupt and minimize communication and make the system less healthy.

Dr. Leaf also indicates there are two types of emotion: fear-based and faith-based.
- <u>Fear-based emotions</u> produce anger, hate, hostility, ill will, bitterness, frustration, fear, unforgiveness, anxiety and worry. When a thought results in negative or fear-based emotion, toxic chemicals are released. When we are primarily negative, we marinate the cells of our bodies in toxic chemicals. This damages the cell defense system and unwanted organisms can enter such as viruses and cancer.
- <u>Faith-based emotions</u> produce love, joy, peace, happiness, kindness, gentleness, self-control, and patience. When thoughts result in positive or faith-based emotion, healthy chemicals are released. When we are primarily positive, cells stay healthy and hold damage and disease at bay.

All brain parts work together to produce a bio-chemical response to thought and emotion. Chemicals travel through the body, influencing systems in 'ordered' sequence. Chemicals, good and bad, affect the circulatory, immune, nervous, and digestive systems. These emotions result in attitudes, which result in behaviors.

Prolonged emotions eventually predominate and take over (either negative or positive). When we control, process and integrate thoughts, we provide healthy environments. In healthy environments, neurons, dendrites and glial work in harmony.

The Heart's Brain

Gary Schwartz and his colleagues at the University of Arizona realized in their study of electroencephalograms (EEG) (1), that neurological or other established communication pathways could explain the complex patterns of heart activity in our brain waves. Their data showed the existence of direct energetic interaction between the electromagnetic field of the heart and that produced by the brain.

The heart is so important that God gave it a 'mini-brain' to be our conscience that would help us determine value—good or bad. When the information seems bad, we can ask God to show us what He wants us to learn. We can look for potential positives in the information as well, thus, He guides our thoughts and decisions. We can remember scripture that can replace the negative messages we receive (see Chapter Eight–Transforming our thought Distortions, and Who Am I?).

> *Therefore, as the Elect of God, Holy and Beloved, put-on Tender Mercies, Kindness, Humility, Meekness, Longsuffering; Bearing with One Another, and Forgiving One Another; if Anyone has a Complaint Against Another; Even as Christ Forgave You, so You Also Must Do.*
> *—Colossians 3:12–13*

Groundbreaking research by *Dr. Candace Pert, called Molecules of Emotion*, (UK: Simon and Schuster, 1997) (1), shows that emotions regulate what you experience as reality. The brain, glands, immune system, in fact, your entire body, is joined together by a wonderful system of peptides. Peptides are bio-chemicals that carry information through the different systems of the body, enabling the brain and the cells of the body to communicate. Emotions and their biological components establish the crucial link between the mind and the body.

The heart can pull every other bodily system into its own rhythm, whatever that may be. When the heart is at peace or filled with love, it communicates harmony to the entire body. And conversely, when toxic emotions have triggered the heart to beat in an irregular way, to beat harder, or to beat faster, the heart communicates the very opposite of peace to the other organs of the body. (Don Colbert, M.D.—*Communication with our heart*) (1))

The Crucial Link

Heart rates tend to send varying messages to the brain and body.
- When a person is fearful, for example, the heart speeds up, sending a signal to the entire body.
- When a person is content and happy, heart rate slows, telling the
- entire nervous system that the person is feeling good.

> *Don Colbert, M.D., in his book* Deadly Emotions *said, "As we learn to communicate with our own heart and release positive feelings of love to our own soul, our heart in turn communicates this message of well-being to our body through the release of hormones and neurotransmitters."* (2)

Prolonged Stress and Trauma System Damage
The Amygdala and Hypothalamus

A chemical messenger in the brain awakens the <u>amygdala</u>, a part of the brain that primes the body for danger which then sets off a myriad of other physical responses. (*Taken from an article* written by *John Futty in the Science Section of The Columbus Dispatch, October 29, 2002* (2). This specific receptor in the <u>limbic system</u> is equipped for responding automatically to any manner of threat.

Other studies show that the <u>hypothalamus</u> signals the adrenal glands to produce more of the hormones <u>adrenaline</u> and <u>cortisol</u> and release them into the bloodstream. These hormones speed up heart rate, breathing rate, blood pressure, and metabolism. Blood vessels open wider to let more blood flow to large muscle groups, putting our muscles on alert. Following are some of the reactions of our bodies to trauma.

Prolonged Stress and Trauma results in Drug Addiction and Drug Related Deaths

Using data from the Centers for Disease Control and Prevention, Statists released a variety of infographics about the opiate epidemic. Here are some highlights:

- Percentage of adults who have heard of opioids but did not know exactly what they were as of 2017: 27%
- In 2017, there were 70,237 deaths from drug overdoses in the U.S. last year which is a record high.
- Overall rates of deaths from overdoses increased 9.6 percent between 2016 and 2017.
- The death rate from synthetic opioids such as fentanyl skyrocketed by 45 percent.
- According to CDC, the age-adjusted rate of drug overdose deaths in the U.S. was 6.1 per 100,000 people in 1999 and that soared to 21.7 in 2017.
- Virginia had the highest death rate per 100,000 inhabitants at 57.8, followed by Ohio (46.3) and Pennsylvania (44.3).

TRAUMA RELATED STATISTICS

SINGLE-PARENT HOMES—Children from single parent homes, especially those with no father influence, have directly resulted in the following:

- 75% increase in teen suicide by overdose
- Rising homicide rates for children
- A majority of rapists, murderers and violent criminals (approximately 70% of adolescent murderers are from fatherless homes)
- Majority of population in the criminal justice system (juvenile and adult)
- A continuing increase in arrests for violent crimes among minors
- An increase in the number of drug-addicted babies
- An increase in drug and alcohol-related problems
- An increase in addiction to pornography
- Increase in sexual abuse of children, affecting their sexual identification
- Men and women growing up with an "orphan spirit".

ABORTION—It is estimated that nearly one million abortions take place annually and more than 55 million abortions have been performed in the U.S. since 1973, based on accumulative data from the two primary sources of U.S. abortion statistics—U.S. Centers for Disease Control (CDC) and Guttmacher Institute.

STATISTICS:
- 1.5% ABORTIONS DUE TO RAPE/INCEST
- 85% Unmarried
- 50% Under 24
- 25% (1/4) of U.S. women will have an abortion by age 45
- 78% Surgical Abortion/ 22% Chemical Abortion
- 60% Have at least one other child
- 40% Have no other children

EPIDEMIC OF SUICIDE—Suicide is a leading cause of death in the United States. According to the Centers for Disease Control and Prevention (CDC) WISQARS Leading Causes of Death Reports, In 2016:
- Suicide was the tenth leading cause of death overall in the US, claiming the lives of nearly 45,000 people.
- Suicide was the second leading cause of death among individuals between the ages of 10 and 35, and the fourth leading cause of death among individuals between the ages of 35 and 54.
- There were more than twice as many suicides (44,965) in the US as there were homicides (19,362).

MENTAL HEALTH FACTS—Common features:
- 83 million Americans have a mental health condition—(18%)
- 9.6 million—Nearly half have co-occurring substance abuse disorder
- 56% of American adults with mental illness did not receive treatment
- In a five-year period, rates of severe youth depression have increased from 5.9% to 8.2%
- Over 1.7 million youth with major depressive episodes did not receive treatment

UNDERAGE DRINKING CLAIMS THE LIVES OF 4,700 PEOPLE UNDER 21 EACH YEAR.

PORNOGRAPHY—Since the rise of the world-wide web, the rise in adult websites sprang up everywhere. As a result:
- 12% of the websites on the internet are pornographic
- Every second $3,075.64 is being spent on pornography
- 40 million Americans are regular visitors to porn sites
- 1in3 women are porn viewers, 70% of men aged18+ visit porn sites in a typical month
- 2.5 billion e-mails per day are pornographic
- 25% of all search engine requests are pornography related
- 34% of internet users have experienced unwanted exposure to porn either through pop-up ads, misdirected links or emails.

Breakdown in Families and Culture Dictate More Single Moms, Children Without Fathers.

- The number of U.S. children living with an unmarried parent jumped from 13% in 1968 to 32% in 2017
- The number of children living with two married parents dropped from 85% in 1968 to 65% in 2017.
- According to the new Pew Research Center analysis of U.S. Census Bureau data, 3% of children are not living with any parents at all.
- Rising numbers of children living with cohabiting or solo parents can be tied to the declines in marriage and the rise in births outside marriage.
- Also, rising divorce rates often result in more children being raised by one parent.

Through faith, we trust in His strength and when we line up our wills with His precepts, we can develop self-control, thus, we can control our thoughts and actions.

If we will take time to process incoming information and allow our heart to discern, instead of reacting to incoming information and acting rashly, we can avoid making decisions that are harmful to us and others. Electrical impulses carrying thought can be held over 48 hours prior to chemical release. This allows us to carefully consider and process them. Over time, we will develop healthy ways to process and respond and develop healthy habits. Or we can develop unhealthy habits and allow our hearts to become hardened.

When experiencing pain, ask God:

- What are you trying to <u>Show</u> me?
- What are you trying to <u>Teach</u> me?
- What <u>Issues of the Heart</u> are you trying to raise through this?
- What are you asking me to <u>Let Go</u> of?
- What is <u>In the Way</u> of my healing?

Self-Control

Even if we control our mental activity, we humans cannot eliminate the flesh and its tendencies toward sin and selfishness. We are made in the image of our creator (Genesis 1:26). When we receive Him into our hearts, His Holy Spirit lives <u>in</u> us. Through faith, we trust in His strength and when we line up our wills with His precepts, we can develop self-control, thus, we can control our thoughts and actions.

If we will take time to process incoming information and allow our hearts to discern, instead of reacting to incoming information and acting rashly, we can avoid making decisions that are harmful to us and others. Electrical impulses carrying thought can be held over 48 hours prior to chemical release. This allows us to carefully consider and process them. Over time, we will develop healthy ways to process and respond and develop healthy habits. Or we can develop unhealthy habits and allow our hearts to become hardened.

SYSTEM DAMAGE DUE TO STRESS AND TRAUMA
Dr. Caroline Leaf, *Who Switched off My Brain* (3)

Circulatory System—what happens:
    Blood pressure increases
    Heart beat becomes rapid
    Arteries restricted (narrowed)
    Artery wall damage (thicken)
    Emotional ache (pain)
    Heart break when toxicity overwhelms
    Fatty plaque rupture & increase in number

Diseases:
Hypertension
Angina
Coronary Artery Disease
Stroke
Cerebrovascular Inefficiency
Aneurysm

Immune System—what happens:
    Generates blood proteins (cytokines)
    Loss of ability to identify real dangers
    Body turns on itself instead of disease

Diseases:
Type 1 Diabetes
Cancer
AIDS
Asthma/Bronchial/Allergy
Skin Diseases
Crohn's Disease
Auto-Immune Disorders
Inflammations
Fibromyalgia
Fatigue
Depression

Central Nervous System—what happens:
    Chemical balance in brain goes haywire

Diseases:
Depression
Phobias/Anxiety
Panic Attacks
Fatigue/Lethargy/Exhaustion
Insomnia
Foggy thinking
Creativity/Memory Loss

Digestive System—what happens:
    Desire for comfort food
    Food/chemicals—poisonous cocktail
    Digestion disrupted

Diseases:
Constipation
Diarrhea
Nausea/Vomiting
Abdominal Cramping
Ulcers
Leaky Gut Syndrome
Irritable Bowel Syndrome

Other—what happens:
    Reproductive Organ Damage
    Growth Hormones Impacted
    Chronic Pain
    Skeletal Weakness
    Viruses invade cells

Diseases:
Fertility Malfunction
Stunted or Abnormal Growth
Muscular Atrophy
Osteoporosis
Arthritis
Virus Infection

Many more aberrations can occur as toxic chemicals circulate, including organ damage. Negative thinking & toxic chemicals can affect life, health, and relationships for a lifetime. Positive thinking & good chemicals can also affect life, health, and relationships throughout life.

Session Two

THE POWER OF THE MIND

Faith and Fear

Faith and *fear* are not just emotions, but spiritual forces with chemical and electrical representation in the body. Consequently, they directly impact bodily function.
- Every emotion result in an attitude. An attitude is a state of mind that produces a reaction in the body and a resultant behavior.
- All negative emotions evolve out of fear.
- All positive emotions evolve out of faith.
- There are sets of molecules of emotion for each of these spiritual forces.

Fear automatically puts the body into stress mode and reaction.
- Examples of fear-based emotions are hate, worry, anxiety, anger, hostility, rage, ill-will, resentment, frustration, impatience and irritation. These produce toxic attitudes which produce toxic responses in the body.
- Anxiety is one of the most toxic emotions that fear produces and can linger long after the threat has come and gone. Anxiety disorders are common and becoming more so.
- Science is now able to demonstrate the links between fear and disease and anxiety and disease through innovative testing and imaging techniques and technology.
- Hate is usually rooted in bitterness, resentment and anger, caused by some grievance.
- Emotions such as hate demand more and more space physically in the brain as well as in the thought life, often crowding everything else out.

Where the mind goes, the health of your body will follow. If your mind is full of anxiety, fear, anger, depression, and guilt, it chronically stimulates the stress response which opens the door for disease to enter the body. When you experience God's peace, the heart communicates peace to every fiber of your being. Each organ experiences His rest.

Post-Traumatic Stress Disorder

<u>Definition</u>: Post-Traumatic Stress Disorder, PTSD, is an anxiety disorder that can develop after exposure to a terrifying event or ordeal in which grave physical harm occurred or was threatened. It is a diagnosis based on symptoms of fear, terror, helplessness, and avoidance of stimuli associated with past trauma. Psychologically speaking, it is a condition that can develop when a person sees or experiences something traumatic, such as:
- Being in a serious car accident or an airplane crash
- Victim of a natural disaster
- Object of an assault like a rape, kidnapping
- Wartime combat
- Participating or witness to violence
- Witnessing a suicide or murder

Some Symptoms are:
- Emotional numbing
- Sleep problems
- Irritability
- Hyper-vigilance
- Depression
- Poor concentration
- Nightmares
- Withdrawal
- Flashbacks
- Recurrent dreams
- Forgetfulness
- Anxiety
- Fatigue
- Intrusive memories

Childhood Trauma Affects Development—(*The Traumatized Child,* 2004, by Margaret Blanstein) (1)

Traumatic events can happen to a child even in the womb—such things as:
- Emotional or physical abandonment by the mother
- Stressful birth
- Shaken Baby Syndrome
- Physical, sexual abuse
- Starvation
- Alienation
- Loss of parent(s)
- Serious accident

When trauma occurs early in life, children do not develop the capacity to:
- Regulate their experiences,
- Calm themselves down when they are upset,
- Soothe themselves,
- Interact in appropriate ways with other people,
- Learn from their behavior (Margaret Blanstein, *The Traumatized Child,* 2004).(2)

2 Corinthians 4:6— *"For God, who commanded the light to shine out of darkness hath shined in our hearts, to give the light of the knowledge of the glory of God in the face of Jesus Christ." said, "Let light shine out of darkness" made His light shine in our hearts to give us the light of knowledge of the glory of God in the face of Jesus Christ."*

Romans 12:2— *"Be not conformed any longer to this world, but be transformed by the renewing of your mind that we may prove what is that good, and acceptable, and perfect will of God."*

SYSTEM DAMAGE DUE TO STRESS AND TRAUMA
Dr. Caroline Leaf, *Who Switched off My Brain* (3)

Circulatory System—what happens:
- Blood pressure increases
- Heart beat becomes rapid
- Arteries restricted (narrowed)
- Artery wall damage (thicken)
- Emotional ache (pain)
- Heart break when toxicity overwhelms
- Fatty plaque rupture & increase in number

Diseases:
- Hypertension
- Angina
- Coronary Artery Disease
- Stroke
- Cerebrovascular Inefficiency
- Aneurysm

Immune System—what happens:
- Generates blood proteins (cytokines)
- Loss of ability to identify real dangers
- Body turns on itself instead of disease

Diseases:
- Type 1 Diabetes
- Cancer
- AIDS
- Asthma/Bronchial/Allergy
- Skin Diseases
- Crohn's Disease
- Auto-Immune Disorders
- Inflammations
- Fibromyalgia
- Fatigue
- Depression

Central Nervous System—what happens:
- Chemical balance in brain goes haywire

Diseases:
- Depression
- Phobias/Anxiety
- Panic Attacks
- Fatigue/Lethargy/Exhaustion
- Insomnia
- Foggy thinking
- Creativity/Memory Loss

Digestive System—what happens:
- Desire for comfort food
- Food/chemicals—poisonous cocktail
- Digestion disrupted

Diseases:
- Constipation
- Diarrhea
- Nausea/Vomiting
- Abdominal Cramping
- Ulcers
- Leaky Gut Syndrome
- Irritable Bowel Syndrome

Other—what happens:
- Reproductive Organ Damage
- Growth Hormones Impacted
- Chronic Pain
- Skeletal Weakness
- Viruses invade cells

Diseases:
- Fertility Malfunction
- Stunted or Abnormal Growth
- Muscular Atrophy
- Osteoporosis
- Arthritis
- Virus Infection

Many more aberrations can occur as toxic chemicals circulate, including organ damage. Negative thinking & toxic chemicals can affect life, health, and relationships for a lifetime. Positive thinking & good chemicals can also affect life, health, and relationships throughout life.

Childhood Trauma

<u>Shaken Baby Syndrome</u>: If a baby experiences severe shaking within the first year of life, results can be:
- Severe and permanent brain injury
- Spinal-cord injuries
- Bleeding in the eyes (retinal hemorrhages)
- Death

Exposure to Trauma from Conception to Age Three:

Trauma at this age exposes the developing brain/body system to what can be termed as "arrested emotional development." In an article by *Post Institute for Family-Centered Therapy* entitled *Getting to the Heart of Healing,* Dr. Bryan Post writes, "The environment of calm interaction between parent and child is necessary for the successful development of the brain/body tools for emotional regulation. When this is absent, the normal and healthy developmental experiences are missed. This absence of calm interaction can result in:

- <u>Chronic stress response</u>. Which, without knowing how to comfort himself, can lead to...
    - <u>Prolonged Stress</u>. The brain and body respond to stress inwardly, which translates cognitively into...
        - <u>Fear</u>, which triggers the <u>Fight</u>, <u>Flight</u>, or <u>Freeze</u> Response.

They don't have the vocabulary to interact in appropriate ways with others and have no way of learning from their behavior. (*The Traumatized Child*, 2004, by Margaret Blanstein)

Behaviors that derive from abuse or neglect, or result in a mental health diagnosis, are not typical child development behaviors.

Developmental Problems

Trauma can affect a child differently at each age level, depending on the developmental stage he is in when the trauma occurs. The following clues indicate a need for "Growing Up Again." Several studies have been made of Dr. Erik Erikson's *Stages of Child Development*. Jean Illsley Clarke and Connie Dawson, authors of *Growing Up Again*, Hazelden Education, 1989, and Dr. Mark Johnson, author of *Spiritual Warfare for the Wounded,* 1992, Servant Publications, identified the following stages and identified characteristics that develop as a result of trauma during each developmental stage. One can look at these characteristics and identify at what stage of development the trauma took place.

Birth to Two Years

<u>Trust vs. distrust issues</u>. When love and nurturance are consistently given, that child learns that it is safe to trust and "okay" to have needs. An unhealthy environment where care and nurturing are withheld or given sporadically, we learn that it is not safe to trust. Our neediness makes us feel vulnerable or unsafe. Some of the characteristics and misbeliefs that develop as a result of arrest at this stage are:

Difficulty in asking for help or emotional support:
- Unable to trust others
- Not knowing what you need, not needing (feeling numb)
- Believing others are more important
- A tendency to focus on others' faults
- A tendency to be guarded and overly sensitive
- An inability to control urges, often resulting in compulsive behaviors
- An inability to be self-disclosing
- A tendency toward pessimism or chronic dissatisfaction
- A tendency toward isolationism
- Generalized fear or anxiety
- Using illness as a reason to be cared for

Two to Four Years

Autonomy vs. Shame and Doubt issues. The focus at this age is separation, moving toward a social and emotional mastery of our immediate environment. Healthy, nurturing parents will encourage us to stand on our own feet. They will provide firm, loving control of the tendency toward anarchy that results from our lack of maturity and provide opportunities to make healthy choices. A sense of confident autonomy develops in such a family. In a detrimental environment, we experience shaming used as a punishment, the suppression of self-expression, and over-control. Developmental arrest at this stage can result in the following characteristics:
- Overdependence on relationships
- Expecting misfortune to follow whenever we feel good
- A fixation on our own improprieties
- A tendency to be "other-related"
- A preference for being told what to do
- An inability to say "no"
- A tendency to live according to "should" and "ought"
- Inappropriate rebellion
- Black and white thinking
- A tendency to be easily dominated
- Chronic worry and self-doubt
- Chronic idealization of others
- A tendency to have love/hate relationships
- Difficulty letting go
- A constant search for heroes or saviors
- Thinking the world revolves around self
- Fear of anger in self or others
- Answering without thinking

Four to Seven Years

<u>Initiative vs. guilt</u>: establishing primary identity, desire to be in control of our destiny. In a healthy family, parents provide us with opportunities to plan and carry out activities. We develop confidence in our ability to plan and attack a task. In an unhealthy environment, we are inhibited from undertaking tasks and experience derision of our abilities in this area.

- An unwillingness to take risks
- The assumption of blame for every failure
- Becoming the classic "underachiever"
- An inability to get anything done or to set goals
- Resistance to new challenges
- Being rigidly moralistic
- Inertia—someone else must always tell us how to get started
- Fear of "rocking the boat"
- Constantly feeling guilty or feeling the need to try harder
- Constant procrastination
- Fear of disapproval, failure, ridicule, or rejection
- Unwillingness to take a leadership role
- Needing others to tell us how to feel
- Constant apologizing
- Perfectionism

Seven to Twelve Years

<u>Industry/structure vs. inferiority issues</u>: great desire to be useful or to produce. During this stage parents need to give clear and systematic instruction, recognize our product or service, and applaud its usefulness. If the family fails to teach healthy ways to relate to adults and children in school and the broader world, then an arrest can occur at this stage.

- Rebellious or antisocial behavior
- Playing it safe, non-productivity, or fear of failing to produce
- Being loud and distracting or being a clown
- Lack of curiosity or desire to learn new things
- Hating to begin new projects
- Poor learning ability
- Compensating for feelings of inferiority by being a braggart or daredevil
- An inability to take criticism
- An inability to complete things, or we sabotage our efforts so that we will have an excuse not to produce
- Compensating by building a reputation for being bright and logical or seen as intellectual
- Feelings of inadequacy or rationalizing our failures
- Constantly second guessing ourselves
- Not wanting anyone to notice us or feeling conspicuous
- Constant feelings of a lack of acceptance
- A constant need to be thinner, prettier, or better looking

Twelve to Eighteen Years
<u>Identity, separation vs. identity diffusion</u>, separation issues. In healthy environments we will have our self-image validated both as a human being and as a male or female. We will be assisted in accepting our weaknesses and will be provided the opportunity to pursue activities in keeping with our strengths. In unhealthy environments, we will have our sense of identity undermined—both as a member of our sex and as a worthwhile human being. An arrest at this stage can result in these behaviors:
- Chronic worrying
- Thrill seeking
- Overachieving
- Compulsiveness, rigidity, or perfectionism
- Feeling a desperate need to be 'right'
- Setting many goals without a long-range plan
- Difficulty getting close to people
- Indecisiveness—fearing a wrong decision so much that we make none
- A critical or cynical attitude
- Becoming fatalists. Feeling 'it's out of my hands'
- A self-concept determined by how well we are "producing"
- Being unable to define what we want or how we fit in
- Having lots of ideas with an inability to put them into action
- Perpetual adolescence or an unwillingness to grow up
- Lack of ambition, being easily distracted, dissatisfied, or bored
- Wanting to be like everyone else

Young Adulthood
<u>Intimacy vs. Isolation</u>; Interdependence vs. Adulthood
When intimacy is fostered, we learn to be committed to a partnership and develop the internal strength to maintain that commitment. An arrest occurs when young adults experience exploitation, abuse, or competitiveness rather than a mutuality of efforts and cooperativeness. Behaviors that tend to develop as the result of an arrest at this stage are:
- Wanting to be everyone's friend but no one's lover
- An inability to wholly give oneself to someone else
- An unwillingness to adapt for the common good or an inability to compromise
- "Hyper" independence
- Feeling "out of control" when attempting to enter a committed relationship
- An unwillingness to settle down
- Feeling that commitment results in being "stuck"
- Difficulty in distinguishing "wanting" from "needing" someone
- Leave home but return several times
- Believing that "giving in" is equal to "giving up"
- Going from one relationship to another
- Continual need to be the "center" of any relationship
- Believing that commitment means forfeiting self
- An unwillingness to ask people for what we need

Arrested Development
Brain research leads us to believe that the amygdala forms while still in utero. The hippocampus, on the other hand, is developing throughout the critical early period of infancy. In this manner, if the environment has been overly stressful and lacks effective parental regulation at an early age:
- The hippocampus becomes stagnated in its growth–hence the term 'arrested emotional development.'
- The amygdala then pours out stress.
- The hippocampus becomes so poorly developed that it is unable to determine to any successful degree, how stressful an event may truly be.
- As a result, the stress and relating fear escalate.
- The rational processes become confused and distorted.
- The amygdala pumps out stress and fear in an uncontrollable manner, and the child is essentially held hostage to his own brain/body system.

Traumatized children do not 'develop' the same as *non*-traumatized children. They exhibit:
- Serious cognitive and gross developmental cognitive and developmental delays
- Impaired communication
- Frustration and anxiety
- Severe behavioral problems such as violent outbursts
- Low reaction threshold
- Anxiety and anger fuel acting-out behavior
- Acting-out behaviors as a result of triggers
- Serious cognitive and gross developmental delays

Abnormal Coping Behaviors
A child develops abnormal behaviors as a means of dealing with his/her pain, frustration and confusion. Below are examples.
- May be prone to violent rages
- May steal from others or hide things
- Encopresis (fecal accidents—repeated passing of stools into places other than the toilet—well past the time of normal toilet training. May result in hiding underwear or smearing feces),
- Anger at the care-giving mother or other children in the home
- Inability to follow rules
- Failure to bond
- Isolation
- Creating a fantasy world
- Lying
- Delayed cognitive functioning
- Lack of perception regarding events
- Lack of strength or knowledge (leading to helplessness)
- Crying to manipulate situations
- Inability to be soothed by or seek out caregiver when in trouble
- 'Checking out' (dissociation / isolation), shutting down

SYSTEMATIC PROCESS FOR RESOLVING UNRESOLVED CONFLICT ETERNALLY (SPRUCE) 🌲

Unresolved Conflict

Most victims of abuse do not seek help on their own for the original injury
- It usually takes a major outburst or eruption that draws the attention of the police, school officials, medical or mental health agencies to get help.
- Lack of training in trauma and abuse often results in little real help.
- The urgency of the immediate problem does not allow for discovery of deeper secrets to be considered or addressed.

Cyclical Thinking

Cyclical thinking is a pattern that involves thought distortions that become beliefs that we act on. Our thoughts lead to emotions which lead to actions. The actions can result in reactions from our environment which can trigger another thought distortion, resulting in actions that bring further negative results, resulting in an affirmation of the original thought distortion or faulty belief. Once a neurological pathway has been paved as a result of repeated stress and traumatic events, it is impossible to alter someone's way of thinking and feeling without help. The beliefs are justified every time the stressor is experienced. They eventually become a habit—then an automatic response. If the faulty beliefs are not identified and changed, the survivor becomes a true believer of their justifications and defenses. The following diagram will help you see the endless flow of cycles that can lock one into a <u>cyclical pattern that keeps repeating itself</u> with every confrontation with conflict. Millie McCarty ©2009, *Why We Can't "Just Get Over It"*.

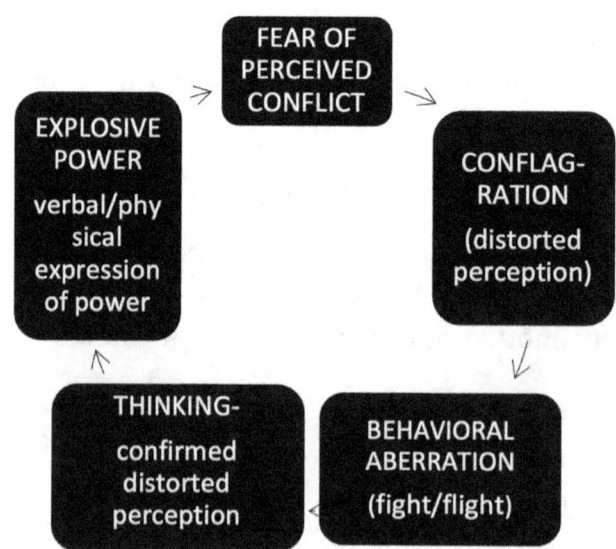

Unresolved Conflict

Persons who have experienced trauma that is accompanied by guilt and shame are most likely to guard these secrets as if they are pots of pure, unspeakable gold as matters of life and death. These secrets usually involve physical, verbal, emotional or sexual abuse, or violence. The generated <u>bitterness, anger, rage, and painful thoughts that never get</u> expressed, <u>poison the system</u>. The result is a festering illness that lives inside and feeds upon tender life tissue, both physical, mental and spiritual, becoming a powerhouse of deadly emotions. Forbidden to express painful emotions, these people press their secret hurts, anger, rage, revenge, and bitterness even deeper until they have all the ingredients (toxic emotions) of a powerful piece of dynamite in their gut.

Fear of Conflict

Most abuse victims have learned to fear conflict of any kind because in their past experience, conflict usually resulted in some form of violence or abuse (e.g., domestic violence, sexual abuse, abandonment, rejection, alcoholic binges and resulting arguments, fights, or other unpleasant or violent exchanges, reminiscent of prior negative experience). This fear of conflict puts them in emotionally disturbing situations with people in authority or greater strength, reminding them of their abusers, the abuse itself, or of the trauma. Just the thought of conflict stirs old cyclical thinking, rooted in a remembrance, which might be triggered by a sound, a mental picture, a smell or touch. Triggers plunge them back to previously painful experiences that generate fear and create conflict in their spirits which <u>sparks a conflagration.</u>

Conflagration

<u>Definition</u>: A destructive fire, usually an extensive one; to burn up; a very intense and uncontrolled fire; a fire extending to many objects, or over a large space; a general burning. When <u>a piece of a memory sets on fire or sparks old frustrations</u>, fears, lies, anger and hate issues, that then connects with distorted or destructive thought patterns, and the mind-body interaction (the brain and the enteric nervous system) can create a conflagration.

Aberration

Definition: A state of condition that is markedly different from the norm; a disorder in one's mental state; an optical phenomenon resulting from the failure of a lens or mirror to produce a good image; the act of wandering; deviation, especially from truth or moral rectitude, from the natural state, or from a type; a partial alienation of reason. *Aberrations* are responsible for imperfections in shape or sharpness of the image; inability to produce a true image; <u>distorted reality.</u> This can cause ongoing or renewed <u>distortions in perception and thought</u>, bringing forth additional or greater toxic outbursts of anger, hatred, frustration and rage, cursing or withdrawal—sometimes causing eruptions, such as hallucinations, convulsions, paralyses of feeling and motion, and the whole procession of symptoms of hysteric disease of body and of mind (J. C. Nemiah, *Early Concepts of Trauma, Memory & Dissociation*, American Psychiatric Press, 1995).

Unresolved Conflict = Explosive Power

Definition: Combustion or explosive power is a complex sequence of (exothermic) chemical reactions between a fuel and an oxidant in which heat is liberated in the form of either a glow or flames. Awakening wounds rooted in distorted perceptions and lies, these lies, and distortions (exothermic chemicals) re-ignite the emotions of hate, rage, and bitterness (oxidant). The combination of toxic thoughts and emotions cause the explosive power that erupts into angry words and behavioral aberrations such as throwing whatever one has in their hand–like dishes or a chair or kicking a hole in the wall. For men, this can be cause for a brutal domestic fight, a bar fight or road rage. This explosive action creates even more conflict, and the Cycle of Cyclical Thinking continues:

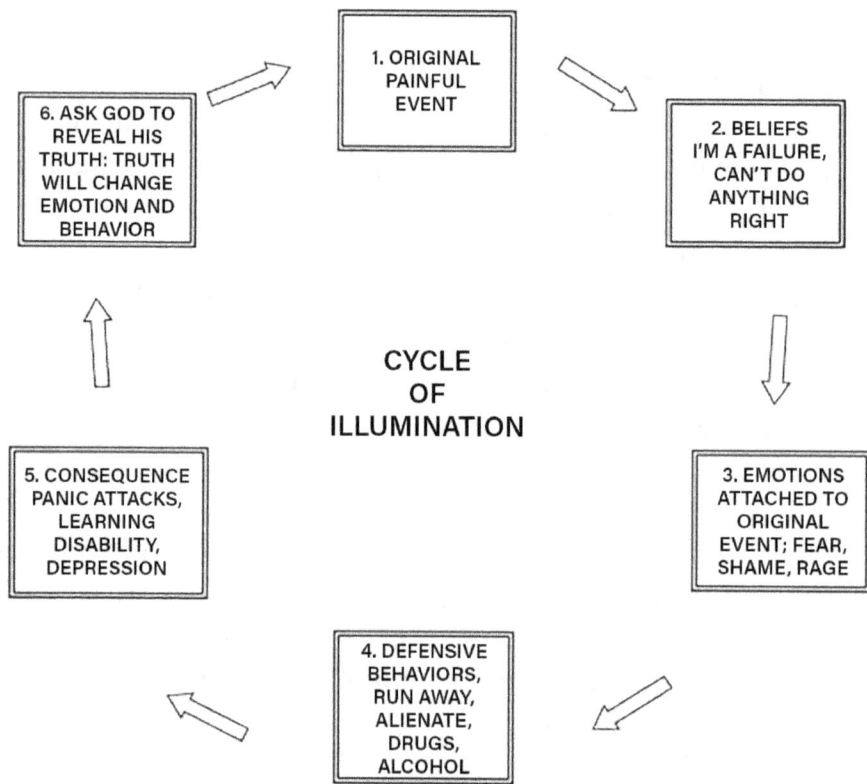

Perceived Conflict → Conflagration → Behavioral Aberration → Cyclical Thinking → Explosive Power ... round and round, like a whirlpool sucking into its whirling motion any floating thought or object toward its center.

<u>**Unresolved Conflict**</u> lies deep within the mind and body. Those who live or work with people with this hidden explosive power within, often find themselves tripping over it or triggering it with what seems to them to be an innocent comment or question and suddenly, they added a straw to the already burning fire and we have combustion.

Social or Relational Issues

Hidden stories from the past and their emotions, distorted thought patterns and behavioral patterns become challenges to communication, transparency, and intimacy. Eruptions of deeply rooted emotions and behavioral reactions result, which create conflictual relationships. This is another example of the elements that make up 'Cyclical Thinking.' The pattern is a bit like an iceberg lying calmly beneath a quiet sea. You are sailing along on calm waters, and then you say one word or do some simple thing, and you trip over that which has lain in stillness under the water—a disaster occurs, and someone is hurt.

Neurological Pathway

- Once a neurological pathway has been paved as a result of repeated stress and traumatic events, it is impossible to alter someone's way of thinking and feeling without help.
- The beliefs are justified every time the stressor is experienced—eventually becoming a habit—then an automatic response.
- Faulty beliefs *must* be identified and changed—otherwise justifications and defenses prevail.

> *The Struggle between Good and Bad, between Tolerance and Intolerance, between Love and Hate, is the Responsibility of Every Individual on this Planet.* —Andrew Newberg, M.D.

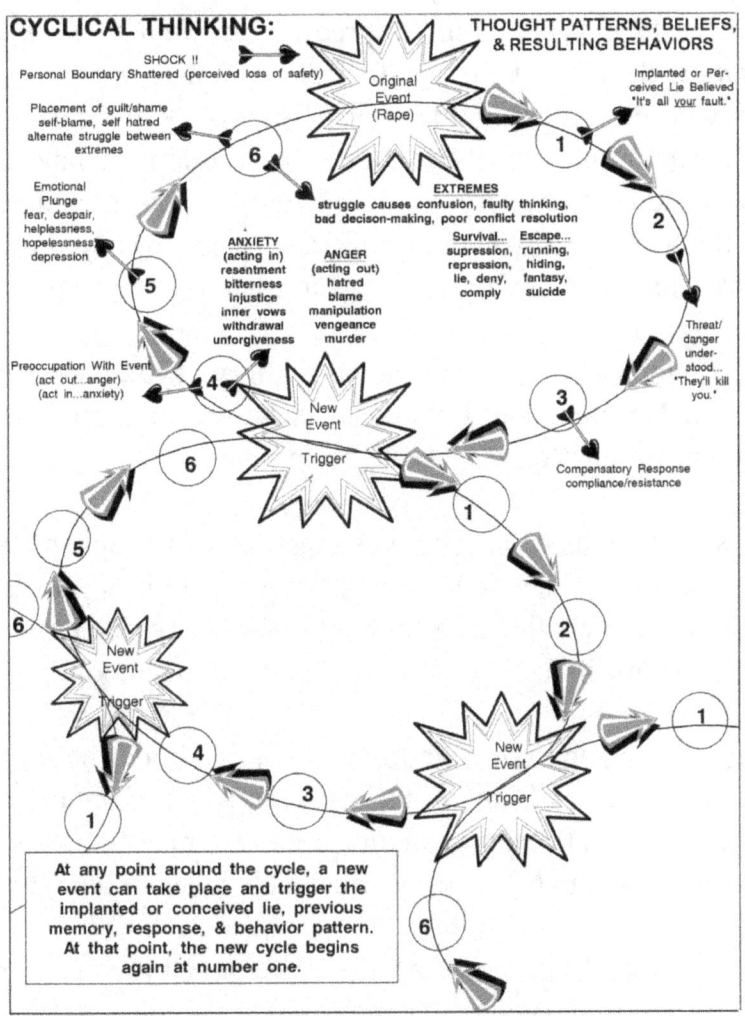

© 2010 by Millie McCarty for *RUTH: Secrets of the Silenced Voices—A Guide to Working with People with Dissociative Identity Disorders.*

Session Three

DEALING WITH ANGRY PEOPLE

The same holds true when dealing with angry people. It is difficult to do, but if you can show compassion for their underlying suffering and pain, their brains will resonate to our kindness. In fact, research has shown that highly empathic people are more likely to respond to an angry expression by smiling. Angry people, however, do not have this ability. In fact, highly aggressive people automatically assume that other people will react to them with anger, and thus they will become even more aggressive, even though no hostility was shown toward them. Andrew Newberg, M.D., (*How God Changes the Brain*, Ballantine Books, NY © 2009).

Resistance from angry people is very common! According to Dr. Henry Cloud and Dr. John Townsend in their book *Boundaries*, which has sold over two million copies, it is not that something has been 'done *to* them,' rather, that someone will not do something 'for them.' Their wish is being frustrated, and they get angry because they have not learned to delay gratification or to respect others' freedom. In Prov. 19:19 it says: *"A man of great wrath shall suffer great punishment; for if thou deliver him, yet thou must do it again."* In fact, Drs. Cloud and Townsend say "the angry person has a character problem. If you reinforce this character problem, it will return tomorrow and the next day in other situations." It is their belief that "it is not the situation that's making the person angry, but the feeling that they are entitled to things from others. They want to control others, and, as a result, they have no control over themselves. So, when they lose their wished-for control over someone, they "lose it." They get angry. Drs. Cloud and Townsend suggest the following steps:

1. <u>Maintain Your Boundaries</u>: The person who is angry at you for setting boundaries is the one with the problem. Maintain your boundaries for it will help them learn what their families of origin did not teach them; to respect other people.

2. <u>Separate Yourself from the Other Person's Anger</u>: Anger is only a feeling, but it can jump across the room to hurt you. It cannot 'get inside' you unless you allow it. Staying separate from another's anger is vitally important. If you either rescue him from it or take it on yourself, the angry person will not get better and you will be in bondage.

3. <u>Do Not Let Anger Be a Cue to Do Something</u>: People without boundaries respond automatically to the anger of others. They rescue, seek approval, or get angry themselves. There is great power in inactivity. Do not let an out-of-control person be the cue for you to change your course. Just allow him to be angry and decide for yourself what you need to do.

4. <u>Set Limits with a Person Who Controls You with Anger</u>: If you are going to set some limits with a person who has controlled you with anger, make sure you have your support system in place. Talk to the people in your support system first and plan. Know what you will say. Anticipate

what the angry person will say and plan your reaction. You may even want to role-play the situation with your group. Then, make sure your support group will be available to you right after the confrontation. Perhaps someone from your support group can go with you. But certainly, you will need them afterward to keep you from crumbling under the pressure.

5. <u>Keep a Loving Stance</u> while "speaking the truth in love." When we get caught up in the "eye for eye" mentality of the law, or the "returning evil for evil" mentality of the world, we will be in bondage. If we have boundaries, we will be separate enough to love.

6. <u>Be Prepared to use Physical Distance and other Limits That Enforce Consequences</u>: One woman's life was changed when she realized that she could say, "I will not allow myself to be yelled at. I will go into the other room until you decide you can talk about this without attacking me. When you can do that, I will talk to you."

These serious steps do not need to be taken with anger. You can empathize lovingly and stay in the conversation, without giving in or being controlled. Search for understanding and remember to empathize, but do not sympathize. Changing your "no" will not help. Offering other options may help. If you keep your boundaries, those who are angry at you will have to learn self-control for the first time, *instead* of "other control" which has been destructive to them. When they no longer have control over you, they will find a different way to relate. But, if they control you with their anger, they will not change. (Taken from *Boundaries,* by Dr. Henry Cloud & Dr. John Townsend, Zondervan, 1992).

Definitions of Cognitive Distortions (from *Feeling Good* by David D. Burns, M.D., Wholecare, 1999)

1. <u>"All or Nothing" Thinking</u>: Person sees things in black or white categories. If his/her performance falls short of perfect, he/she sees it as a total failure.

2. <u>Over-Generalization</u>: Person sees a single negative event as a never-ending pattern of defeat. "I'm always doing that."

3. <u>Mental Filter</u>: Person picks out a single negative detail and dwells on it exclusively so that his/her vision of all reality becomes darkened—like placing one drop of dye in a cup of water—the whole cup of water is colored. Likewise, by focusing on one negative detail, one can miss out on any good in the event.

4. <u>Disqualifying the Positive</u>: Will reject all positive experience by insisting that it doesn't count—can then maintain a negative belief that is contradicted by every-day experiences; false expectations seem real.

5. <u>Jumping to Conclusions</u>: Makes a negative interpretation even though there are no definite facts that can convincingly support the conclusions.

   i. He/she is sure someone is thinking negatively of him/her.

   ii. Anticipates that things will turn out badly and feels convinced the prediction is already an established fact. There are no definite facts that can convincingly support the conclusions.

6. <u>Magnification</u> (catastrophizing) <u>or Minimization</u> (dismissing): Person exaggerates the importance of things—his or her mistake or someone else's achievements, or vice versa.

7. <u>Inappropriately Shrinking or Exaggerating Concepts</u>: Like a pair of binoculars—dependent upon the lens you look through, you may minimize the object you are examining, or magnify it.

8. <u>Emotional Reasoning</u>: Assumes the negative emotions necessarily reflect the way things are. I feel it, therefore it must be true.

9. <u>'Should' Statements</u>: Trying to motivate self with 'should' or 'should nots.' Example: Telling yourself, "I should work on this," but then not doing anything. In more severe situations, "I <u>should</u> be whipped or <u>should</u> be dead." But when action does not match the 'should/should not' message, guilt results.

10. <u>Labeling or Mislabeling</u>: Describing an event or person with language that is highly colored and emotionally loaded. Best expressed as an extreme form of overgeneralization. Instead of describing the error, the person attaches a negative <u>label</u> to him/herself, such as, "I'm always a loser," or attaches it to someone else, "He's useless."

11. <u>Personalization</u>: Sees self as the cause of some negative event for which, in fact, he/she was not primarily responsible. Example: "My children have failed and it's all my fault."

The Mind: A Battleground between Good and Evil
- Toxic thoughts deplete your body and mind of health
- Good thoughts create health in your body

"You can choose to be bitter or better!"

Free Will—You Choose
The *corpus callosum* and *frontal lobe* areas are the parts of the brain that are uniquely involved in this free will process. We can choose to ignore and deny our thoughts or we can choose to:
- Access them
- Explore them
- Analyze them
- Change them

Thoughts—The Root of Pain
Victims of abuse, whether it is physical, verbal, sexual, psychological or emotional, have many <u>distortional thoughts</u>. These thoughts are the roots of much pain, bitterness, unforgiveness, hatred, revenge, helplessness and hopelessness. We see the signs of abuse:
- In the victims' physical demeanor
- In their interaction with others
- How they talk about themselves

Looking back at our life, our memories of what really happened may be distorted or colored by our perception. In our lifetime, we accumulate many beliefs that are the enemy's way of weighing us down so we cannot move freely in the will of God. Many people are laden with distortions that are such a burden they are always walking under a heavy load of guilt and shame. Most of us are unaware of the thoughts we tell ourselves.

If we would listen to what we are confessing with our mouth, we would identify deeply rooted distorted thoughts such as:
- I am always wrong
- I can't handle this any more
- I'm going crazy
- I'm just a misfit

Repeated phrases daily become part of our belief system, thus become part of our identity.
- Thoughts create our mood. When we experience a fear-based emotion, we will feel depressed, and our thoughts will be characterized by negativity. A negative thought linked to emotional turmoil will be distorted.
- Our thoughts can change who we are. Dr. Leaf's book, *Who Switched off My Brain?* describes a process whereby we can control our thought life.

Four Rules for Controlling Your Thought Life
- Understand how a thought forms, how it grows in your brain, stores memories and ultimately how it affects your health, whether positively or negatively.
- Actively analyze. Use your brain's natural "sifter," the glial cells, that increases conscious awareness of your thoughts and feelings and leads the process of actively analyzing incoming information and thoughts.

- Make a conscious decision to accept the thought if it is good for you OR reject it if it is bad for you.
- Deal with the emotional strongholds—toxic thoughts, emotions and the chemicals they generate that negatively affect the free flow of important electrochemical processes in your brain and build strong memory.

Flashbacks and Triggers

Flashbacks and triggers come at uncertain times, however. Memories are often triggered by family anniversaries and normal transitions in family life such as losses.

Flashbacks and triggers give us good opportunity to begin the process of becoming aware of our thoughts and emotions, to examine them and trace them back to the original traumatic event. By doing this, we can identify and change our thought distortions. Flashbacks contain the memory pieces brought together by the physiological, mental, emotional memories into which the lies or distortions are planted. Healing the memory cannot be complete without discovering the lie or distortion hidden within. Following are steps to guide you through this process.

A. The emotions from flashbacks will usually match the emotions we have experienced in previous life experiences. Flashbacks are our recorded "emotions" or "echoes" of past memories which give us clues as to what is hidden within which we have feared to remember or discuss. We hide them so deeply that we forget about them until something triggers our senses and provides an "echo" or repeated memory.

B. Thought distortions are also evident in the flashback which contains portions of the original event. Once God reveals the original memory, He can also show us how we interpreted what happened and the lies or distortions we believed. I remember a 45-year-old female client who had been in counseling all her life. In and out of foster homes as a child, in and out of treatment centers as a youth and under psychiatric care all her adult life, she always spoke so lovingly of her mother and father. Yet, the truth was that they had been alcoholics and the children were removed from the home several times because of domestic violence. The client had heard something about her father from her siblings and a memory surfaced that she did not want to face. She shared the original shock and dismay that her dad would do such a thing.

C. It is important to identify emotions rather than rejecting them and trying to run from them, it is important to <u>identify them, acknowledge them, and analyze them</u>. Our tendency is to run from our fear and pain rather than facing it. However, refusing to look at it or denying that it is there only prolongs the healing process. If we follow and recall the emotion held within the flashback, the Lord will show us the original memory and bring healing. When we seriously pay attention to incoming information, we activate the corpus callosum, which in turn passes the information into the memory. We are then able to analyze and assess whether this information is helpful or harmful, and store it accordingly as a good, healthy memory. A similar process happens when you focus your mind by meditating on specific thoughts or information. The most valuable coping mechanism you can develop is how to consciously deal with your thoughts, actively accepting some and rejecting others.

D. Follow the emotion to the original experience and connect with the distorted thought planted in your mind by the event. Since God is our creator and sees all and knows all, He already knows the root of our pain or discomfort, which holds our fears, shame and guilt. If we ask God, He will take us directly to the original memory, because He was there. He will show us the exact situation which brought that thought and feeling into existence.

E. Examine the thought distortion considering reality. God will show you every aspect of the trauma as you experienced it and reveal the perception you had at that time. As an adult, you will be able to re-evaluate the truthfulness of your perception, and God will reveal aspects to you that you would have had no way of knowing. What He reveals to you will give you an understanding of reality which will clarify many distorted perceptions.

F. Recognize that the current emotion is connected to the thought distortion. Bio-chemicals make possible dialogue between the conscious, cognitive level and the sub-conscious level. This interconnected, psychosomatic network of emotion and reason has its own peculiar make-up. It is comprised of the circulatory, nervous, endocrine, immune and gastrointestinal systems and communicates every nanosecond via peptides and receptors in cells.

G. Examine thought distortions considering the reality and a choice is made to either believe the truth or continue believing the distortion. It is positive affirmation that replaces bad memories with supportive ones. You literally build a new network of new memories over the old. Positive affirmation is the beginning of changing your thought processes to detoxify the brain (remove the toxins resulting from distortional thoughts), and all the different areas of the brain keep busy doing their own specific tasks.

H. Replace the distorted belief with the Truth, the fear and anxiety will be replaced with peace and understanding. Once God reveals the original memory, He can also show us how we interpreted what happened and the lies or distortions we believed.

We can use this process with every painful memory we have. As stated previously, within each painful memory is the seed of the distortion the enemy wants us to believe. God knows the truth and as His light is shed on the truth, the distortion is dispelled, HE will replace it with His truth, and we are free of the pain.

Nervous System—Main Target of Toxic Thoughts

The central nervous system is a main target on the pathway forged by your toxic thoughts and emotions. Research shows:

- The constriction of blood vessels causes migraines and painful back spasms from reduced blood and oxygen flow to muscles.
- This causes feelings of numbness and pins and needles in your extremities.
- Over time, this constriction leads to a buildup of toxic waste in the muscles, which may be variously diagnosed as fibromyalgia (fibrositis) or repetitive stress injury.
- Once your body is truly in stress mode and the cortisol is flowing.
- Dendrites start shrinking and even falling off.
- The chemical balance in your brain then goes haywire creating confusion.

Immune System Problems

Toxic waste generated by your toxic thoughts and emotions can cause the following problems in the immune system:

- Migraines
- Numbness in extremities
- Type 1 diabetes
- Cancer
- Asthma
- Allergies
- Skin problems (eczema, itching, redness, psoriasis)
- Autoimmune disorders (such as lupus and rheumatoid arthritis)
- Inflammation
- Fibromyalgia
- Chemical imbalance

Chemical Imbalance in the brain can also cause:

- Depression
- Phobias
- Panic attacks
- Fatigue
- Lethargy
- Exhaustion
- Insomnia
- Anxiety
- Foggy thinking
- Lack of creativity
- Headaches (migraines)
- Poor memory

Seven Factors in Reversing Thoughts and Behaviors

Dr. Joe Dispenza says in his book, *Evolve Your Brain,* © 2007, it is mainly because our thoughts and behaviors become automatic, unconscious, that change is uncomfortable. He identifies several factors that must happen for us to change who we have become to become who God wants us to be:

>We <u>Think</u> the Way We <u>Feel</u>,
>>   <u>Feel</u> the Way We <u>Think</u>; therefore,
>>>   To <u>Change</u> the Way we <u>Feel</u>,
>>>>   We Must <u>Change</u> the Way We <u>Think</u>.

- We must TRANSCEND all things that keep us from becoming a separate entity
- We must develop a RELATIONSHIP with the Higher Intelligence (God)
- We must be INTENT (focused) about what we want
- We must SURRENDER to the Greater Intelligence
- We must think GREATER than our environment
- We must think INDEPENDENT of our environment
- We must think GREATER than our feelings

Reversing the Process

In order for change to happen, we must first:
- Recognize the need for change—(This way is not working, I must change.)
- Identify at what point you lost your identity. (The point of violation.)
- Believe in the thoughts more than feelings. (I am *able* vs. I am *helpless*.)

The Change Process

It is very important that we learn how to take time to find a place for quiet meditation and prayer essential to quiet the emotional center. Once we begin to contemplate and focus on our goal, the frontal lobe holds the thought while the rest of the brain makes a new pattern. The body has been conditioned to control the mind, rather than the mind controlling the body. Therefore, the body is hard-wired and to bring about change, we must force the brain to think and choose to act differently in the same environment. Let's look at each of these six components that lead to change.

Quiet Meditation and Prayer

Finding a time and a place for quiet meditation and prayer is essential to quiet the emotional center.

Focus on the Goal (new behavior and actions)

Once we begin to contemplate our goal, the frontal lobe holds the thought while the rest of the brain makes a new pattern.

Force the Brain to Think and Choose to Act Differently

The body has been conditioned to control the mind, rather than the mind controlling the body. Therefore, the body is wired for survival in our environment, and to bring about change, we must force the brain to think and choose to act differently in the same environment.

Inhibit the Old Thoughts

Refuse to walk in agreement with the old, distorted thinking and lies. When we inhibit the old thoughts, the chemicals respond and the body revolts because the mind is no longer sending the same signals to the body. With consistent thought change, the neurons break away and the body becomes conditioned to follow new thoughts.

Rehearse

Just as we learn by repetition in school, if we can picture in our mind the goal we want to achieve, and rehearse in our mind how we are going to change our thoughts and actions, the brain will:
- Make new connections
- Grow new circuits
- Establish new connections with neurons

Surrender the Old in Order to Acquire the New

It is our will that allows the mind and body to work together. Dr. Joe Dispenza says, "Be creative, forget about yourself." Trust the process and something greater will happen. The speed with which our bodies change depends on whether we have declared our intentions, or, if they have remained undeclared. Old messages are hard-wired, unconscious thoughts and reactions that must be unseated and replaced with healthy, productive ones.

Another Research Project Conducted by Dr. Fred Luskin, Director of the Stanford Forgiveness Project at Stanford University. In a related study, levels of emotional hurt plummeted nearly 40 percent in one week of forgiveness training, and depression declined significantly as well. Participants reported a statistically significant increase in their feelings of physical vitality and general well-being, and 35 percent of the people in the study said they felt "less distress."

> *When Chemical Changes Take Place, Moods Change, Temperaments Change and Personalities Change.*

Session Four

TREE OF BONDAGE VS. TREE OF FREEDOM

"Make a tree good and its fruit will be good or make a tree which bringeth not forth its fruit will be bad for a tree is recognized by its fruit." **Matthew 12:33**

"The ax is laid unto the root of the trees therefore, every tree that does not produce good fruit is hewn down, and cast into the fire." **Matthew 3:10**

"For thou has possessed my reins; thou hast covered me in my mother's womb. I will praise thee; for I am fearfully and wonderfully made: marvelous are thy works; and that my soul knoweth right well. My body was not hid from thee when I was made in secret and curiously wrought in the lowest parts of the earth. I praise you because I am fearfully and wonderfully made; your works are wonderful. My frame was not hidden from you when I was made in the secret place. When I was woven together in the depths of the earth, your eyes saw my unformed body. All the days ordained for me were written in your book before one of them came to be." **Psalm 139:13-16**

Each child's life is like a tapestry in the hands of God, weaving every circumstance of his life into the fabric and pattern He desires for each child. We grieve today especially over the lives of our children whose spiritual well-being is sacrificed to the idols of this paganistic world. Most of the mental health and human service agencies are overloaded with cases of child abuse and neglect fostered by parents who are on drugs or alcohol or have themselves been abused and respond in like manner to their children.

God instructed parents to impress His teachings upon their children by talking about them at home and modeling them for their children. As a Christian nation, our first schools were Christian schools where the focus was on teaching our children to read the Bible and the guidelines for living were from God's Word. Discipline was used to bring the child's will in line with God's, not to punish or destroy, but to build character in the child.

We all know that authority and discipline can be abused when the parents themselves are not under the authority of God or are not in control of their own emotions. However, without proper guidance and teachings, children are like rudderless ships, blown and tossed by the winds of the world. God's Word is like a rudder to guide them.

Many people who come for healing were abused sexually, physically, emotionally, and psychologically. We are told in the third chapter of James about the power of the tongue to either build up or destroy. In this chapter, we will talk about the lies that mold and shape people's lives.

"Reckless Words Pierce the Heart Like A Sword, But the Tongue of The Wise Brings Health."
—*Proverbs 12:18*

It is the words and actions written on the hearts of our children that guide them in their life's path. Some homes are fertile soil for healthy, wholesome children to grow and thrive. Other homes are like minefields where hidden bombs are ready to explode in their face and destroy their lives. Homes that provide acceptance, love and a sense of protection including security will usually produce healthy children who know how to handle life's situations with wisdom. Others who have to struggle to survive in a world filled with rejection, hatred and depravity will be marred and given little with which to thrive. It is only by God's grace that some children survive. Of the survivors, many have numerous scars that takes their lives down a twisted path that leads to disastrous results. Others, with God's help, rise above their circumstances and live lives that influence the world in very positive ways.

God is in the business of helping children survive these unbearable situations. The book entitled *"A Child Called "It"* by Dave Pelzer (Health Communications, Inc. Deerfield Beach, Fla. 1995) is his personal account of one of the most severe child abuse cases in California history. It is a true story of being singled out by his alcoholic mother to be brutally beaten and starved to the point of death, and his remarkable unyielding determination to live. This is an unbelievable story of how God breathed His strength and desire for life into a child who was in near-death abuse situations. God placed in him something that gave him the ability to survive and rise above all the abuse. God does not come down and snatch the child away from the parent or the abuser, but He does come. He does a work within the soul and spirit. The book of Isaiah tells us about God's provision for the wounded.

> *"I, even I, am he that comforteth you: Who are you that you fear a man that shall die, and of the son of man which shall be made as grass; and forgettest the Lord thy maker, that hath stretched forth the heavens, and laid the foundations of the earth; and hast feared continually every day because of the fury of the oppressor, as if he were ready to destroy? And where is the fury of the oppressor as if mortal men. the sons of men who are but grass, that you forget the Lord your Maker, who stretched forth the heavens and laid the foundations of the earth, that you live in constant terror every day because of the wrath of the oppressor, who is bent on destruction? For where is the fury of the oppressor? The captive exiles will soon be set loosed; that he should not die in the pit, nor that his head shalt fail they will not die in their dungeon, nor will they lack bread. For I am the Lord your God, who churns up the sea so that its waves roar—the Lord Almighty is his name. I have put my words in your mouth and covered you with the shadow of my hand—I who set the heavens in place, who laid the foundations of the earth, and who say to Zion 'You are my people.'"* **Isaiah 51:12-16**

We find roots of bondage are sown in early childhood, often in the womb. Studies have shown that the emotional, physical, and mental health of the mother while carrying the child in her womb can influence the child's development. When a mother does not want the child or contemplates abortion, the child senses the mother's emotional detachment and suffers rejection in the womb. Children who are adopted have an innate sense of losing the mother who carried them for nine months and have to re-bond with the new mother. The sense of separation from the birth mother is registered in the soul of the child.

When a child has difficulty finding that safety, security, and acceptance necessary for normal and healthy development, seeds of frustration and anger are planted in his spirit. With sustained neglect of nurturing, this can develop into a focus on self. When these early needs go unmet, there is a constant gnawing away at the inner self. The child feels something is missing—a part of him is not like everyone else. The constant looking within to examine self-results in a constant self-evaluation and a perception that they are not acceptable or lovable like other children. They experience jealousy and envy over others' obvious acceptance, deepening their anger and depression. These self-perceptions lead to the development of a sense of shame and guilt that they surround with walls of defenses to protect them from further emotional injury.

TREE OF BONDAGE VS. TREE OF FREEDOM

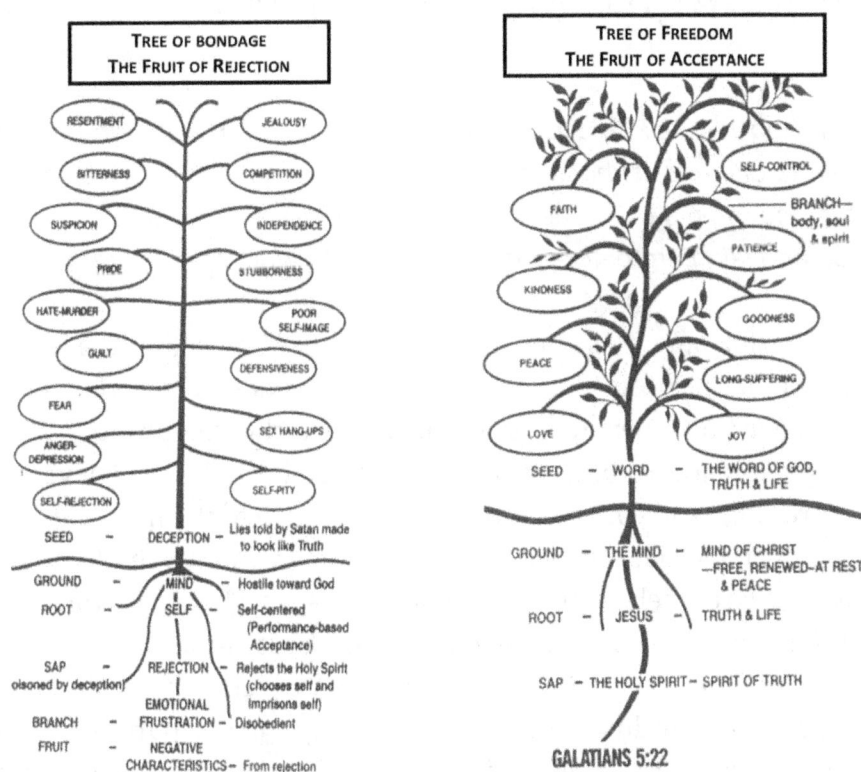

"Make a tree good and its fruit will be good or make a tree bad and its fruit will be bad, for a tree is recognized by its fruit." —Matthew 12:33

(Source Unknown)

FROM DARKNESS INTO HIS LIGHT

"But you are a chosen generation, a royal priesthood, an holy nation, a peculiar people belonging to God, that you may shew forth the praises of him who hath called you out of darkness into his marvelous light. 1 Peter 2:9

The mind is the playground of the enemy. Each of us is born in God with His DNA, and a potential of health and wholeness, a knowing of right and wrong. When working with sexual abuse victims, we rarely meet victims of abuse who did not know that what was being done to them was wrong. It stirred something in them that told them it was wrong, just as surely as it was hurtful. Yet often because what is being said or done is by an adult, one in whom their very survival exists, the inner knowing is defiled, and the knowledge of truth is twisted. With regular conditioning or programming by philosophies, attitudes, and beliefs that are predominant around us, we can quickly begin to believe the lie to be the truth. In fact, we are told, that in the latter times,

> *"Many will come in My name, claiming, 'I am He,' and will deceive many."* **Mark 13:6**

We, as believers in God, have a gauge to identify the lies we are being told…The Bible. It is our plumb line, so to speak that gives us a gauge with which to discern truth from a lie. God himself is **TRUTH**, and His Word conveys truth. When His LIGHT is shed on our beliefs, it is like a two-edged sword. Hebrews 4:12–13 says…

> *"The word of God is quick and powerful. Sharper than any double-edged sword, it piercing even to dividing asunder of soul and spirit, and joints and marrow; it discerns the thoughts and intents of the heart. Nothing is hidden from God's sight. Everything is uncovered and laid bare before the eyes of him to whom we must give account."*

Mind renewal means transforming those lies into truth so we can walk in the freedom and peace that truth brings. It is the lies that begin to change our self-image and over years become strongholds that hold us back from using our God-given identity to move forward with our life. We learned earlier about the Developmental Stages and how traumatic events at each of those stages of development can hinder us from developing the core skills and cognitions necessary to move to the next step. Modern research has demonstrated that all learning is neurological, and we become who we "think" or "believe" we are. Our beliefs determine how we see ourselves, and we act on that belief. The longer the lie has been embedded in our mind, the more intensified the imprint on our beliefs about ourselves, our family and our world.

Sometimes we wonder where certain behaviors and beliefs come from and wonder how they became so predominant. Most of our dominant imprints come from our parents. The rest come from life experiences. Fearful imprints program us for future fearful thought patterns and behaviors. We look at a child and wonder why they are anxious or fearful. Fear of a certain subject or object is an intangible force that increases unless the thought patterns and beliefs are identified and managed. A child who has been frightened by a dog will experience the same emotions the next time he or she sees a dog unless someone helps the child change the fear of dogs through a positive experience that will counteract the bad experience that created the fear. Children do not know how to do this for themselves. They must be taught by a calm, comforting, caregiver who will help the child re-experience this life experience which will transform the child's perception of a dog. If fear goes uncontrolled, it will become a predominant controlling factor.

Our feelings are lodged in our hippocampus, a part of the brain that holds memories. Therefore, fears stay with us and hinder us from moving forward in our growth. The emotions we feel in situations that cause fear, panic, are often triggered by stored up emotions from experiences we have had before. The emotions are often a clue to what is hidden within; things we have feared to remember or discuss. We hide them so deeply that we forget about them until something triggers our senses and provides an echo of the memory.

How many of us know ourselves well enough to be able to manage ourselves significantly to oversee our own emotions? If you don't know how to control your thoughts and emotions, you will be preoccupied with them, and the fearful emotions attached to them. If you don't manage your own thoughts and emotions, so to speak, other voices will control you. How many of us know our own mind and can speak for ourselves? How many of us know what our life purpose is? Only when we are aware of our thoughts, feelings, and can express those out loud, do we have a voice. If we don't have a voice, how will we be able to fulfill our life purpose?

ELEMENTS THAT MAKE UP THE CYCLE OF DYSFUNCTION

A. **PAINFUL MEMORY**: A young boy was born into a family of seven generations of firemen. Strong, tough, firemen who were considered "heroes" in the eyes of their family and city. When this little boy began to demonstrate weakness or tenderness, his father would humiliate him by saying things like "how is a sissy like you ever going to be a fireman?" "How do you expect to be a brave fireman if all you do is whine and cry?" "Come on boy! Toughen up! Firemen can't be "softies"! When he displeased his father, he would be yelled at, and if he did something wrong, his father would "teach" him by whipping him.

B. **BELIEFS**: He saw himself as a failure, could not do anything right, weak, soft, must stay away from home or be beaten and shamed. Believed he would never succeed, certainly would never be the eighth family fireman.

C. **EMOTIONS:** By the age of five he felt unsafe at home, was having panic attacks when Dad was home. He stuttered and was put into special education classes. Felt alienated, avoided intimacy. Full of fear, hate, shame, guilt and rage.

D. **BEHAVIOR:** By the age of ten he was staying away from home all day, not wanting to be there when Dad was there. Wandered the neighborhood, experienced rages at the drop of a hat. Got into drugs, alcohol, sex.

E. **CONSEQUENCES:** Early childhood panic attacks, stuttering, learning disabilities, DUI, drug treatment, pregnancy/abortion.

Dan's life was a mess until his brother encouraged him to enter the training program at the Fire Department and give it a try. After winning many awards for his heroic acts as a fireman, nearly 18 months till retirement, he was depressed and ready to commit suicide. His "failure" to be brave and strong was more than he could handle. At 55 years of age, Dan came to one of our classes for prayer so he wouldn't do what his mind was telling him to do. Below is his Cycle of Dysfunction we drew on the white board that day.

DIAGRAM: CYCLE OF DYSFUNCTION

If we have been taught since childhood that we are a child of God, that we belong to God's family, that God has a purpose for our lives, and it is written in His Book of Life,, and that God is with us and loves us, we will most likely be free to move in our gifting and flow from developmental stage to developmental stage without missing a beat. Those who have grown up fearing for their safety and security, believe themselves to be unwanted, unloved, and rejected, see themselves as "everybody's problem", "not good enough", "a failure" and life experiences prove repeatedly that they are unsafe and uncared for. For people experiencing this kind of childhood, it will be difficult for them to move freely from stage to stage, and will experience inadequacy, insecurity, failure, etc. that will cause them to develop defense mechanisms like explaining, withdrawing, blaming, procrastination, lying, making excuses, justifying, etc., identifying their weaknesses rather than strengths.

Our state of being has an infectious dominating factor that takes up residence in our mind. Anger and hatred will replace peace and joy. Envy and jealousy will replace generosity and trust. Anger, if given space will become a predominant state and eventually overtake your entire being. Children will defend their lives one way or another. These defense mechanisms become a way of life until we examine them to see the root lie, they are based on. See Dan's defense mechanisms on the next page.

DAN'S DEFENSE MECHANISMS
ALIENATION / WITHDRAWAL
ATTACKING / ACQUIESCING
BLAMING / SILENCE
PERFECTION / PROCRASTINATION
LYING / MANIPULATING
SELF-MEDICATION

The consequence of this cycle of thinking is physical and emotional impairment such as attachment issues, anxiety, addictions, self-regulatory problems, aggression, social helplessness, eating disorders, and re-victimization, among others. These emotional problems lead to system damage such as circulatory problems, coronary artery disease, immune system diseases, Type 1 diabetes, and cancer. The price Dan had paid for all his trauma was problems in his marriage, anxiety, addictions, self-regulatory problems, aggression, suicidal thoughts and social helplessness. These emotional problems lead to system damage such as circulatory problems, coronary artery disease, immune system disease, etc.

MULTIPLE DOMAINS OF IMPAIRMENT
a. Self-regulatory problems, attachment issues, anxiety, and affective disorders
b. Addictions
c. Aggression, social helplessness, eating disorders
d. Dissociative, cardiovascular, immunological disorders
e. Sexual disorders
f. Re-victimization

SYSTEM DAMAGE
a. Circulatory problems
b. Coronary Artery Disease
c. Immune system Diseases
d. Type 1 Diabetes
e. Cancer—when the body turns on itself instead of the disease

Our life experiences prepare us to see ourselves in one of two states: empowered or disempowered. In a given event (car accident, argument, disappointment), based upon your background and programming, you will experience a thought, interpretation and action in a microsecond. Those who are programmed with negative thoughts and beliefs will act upon the beliefs and interpretations they have been programmed to believe with repetitive negative results. Those who have been programmed with love, encouragement and truth will feel secure in making right choices and act accordingly.

DISEMPOWERED
Dan saw himself as DISEMPOWERED. At 45 years of age, on Nov. 11, 2001, Dan who was a fireman, was called to an office building to check on a call. As he walked into the office building, dozens of people were standing around a large TV set watching as a plane flew into one of the Twin Towers in New York City, then another. People were jumping out of the building, crying, screaming, panicking, and firemen were carrying people out, fighting against the fire and smoke. People in the room were hysterical. Dan sank to the floor in an absolute panic. Sweat covered his face, tears filled his eyes, his heartbeat like a drum; he could hardly breath. Dan didn't know what hit him, but he went back to the office and told his boss he wanted a desk job; that he could no longer handle being a firefighter. His boss considered that, but the next day sent him out to check on a dog bite. He found a little girl who had been bit by a dog who caught her jugular vein and bled to death. He froze, unable to do anything. He could not pull himself out of it. He was numb, speechless. He went back to the office and told his boss again that he wanted a desk job, and for the past ten years Dan had been working at a desk job. A man who had won many awards for his heroic acts of saving lives. He would just sit it out until retirement.

On the day Dan called his wife for help, she was at one of our seminars, and her big concern that day had been her husband—Sept. 11, 2011—the tenth anniversary of 9-11, the bombing of the Twin Towers in New York. One half hour before class was over, Dan called, saying he was considering suicide, and asked if he would come, if we would pray with him. We said "yes". When Dan arrived, we had him tell us what was going on. That is when Dan told the story of his experience on Sept. 11, 2001. When he recounted how he saw himself as a failure, and his wife is saying "but you won all these awards", we asked him where he got the idea, he was a failure. That is when Dan immediately recounted all the way his father had programmed him to see himself that way.

As I listened to Dan, one of my interns drew the Cycle of Dysfunction on the white board on the wall. When we could see the cycle and we shared with Dan how his fears, shame, his panic attacks, as well as his physical and emotional problems were all based upon his beliefs about himself. I asked him if he would like to hear what God thought about him. He said "Yes". We prayed "God, Dan sees himself as a failure, as a weak person, ashamed of his failures and really hates himself. Would you show Dan how you see him?" Dan listened for the voice of God, and God said to him "The reason you are a good fireman is because of your compassion." Then God said, "I like the person I created you to be." Dan broke down in tears, and his body shook with relief as every ounce of fear, stress, guilt, shame and hatred fell off his body. His legs and body shook with relief from the released pressure of trying to be someone he was not created to be. Dan was set free that day and walked out of that room a changed man, a changed husband and father.

Renewing the mind is physiological, but it is also spiritual. God created our mind and neurological system to be interconnected in such a way that we can shift our state of mind in a heartbeat. Your response to stimuli depends upon the interpretation you give the event. The most successful way to break out of your current state is to adjust your thoughts first, which then will change your feelings. That is because your thoughts program your body to act in a certain way, and your body is so programmed for your disposition that you will automatically respond to your programming. Changing your physiology means changing your thoughts which will change your feelings. Determining to change the way you think will change your programming which will ultimately change your actions.

If your physiology speaks of love and caring, your actions will build relationships and pull people together. If it speaks of anger and rejection, a different message will be communicated...such as strife and division, which alienates. Speak peace to your body, and your body will communicate peace and you will change your environment. Your spirit has authority over the environment. If there is strife in a room, strife comes into you. Your state is like an influence. You can attract or repel depending on your predominant state. Strife will repel peace. Research has proven that we can control our thoughts and our emotions, but we must become aware of our thoughts and feelings, examine them, analyze them and determine which ones we desire to keep, and which need to be replaced.

Most conceptions whether negative or positive are built on past experiences which form our memories. Renewing our minds should not be understood as the removal or changing of the memory, but rather the reinterpretation of the memory by replacing the embedded lie with the truth. Jesus knows all things and will shed His light upon the lie to disengage it and replace it with the truth. Shame and guilt are merely the emotions that match the belief we embrace. This is how the enemy keeps us in bondage to the sin: by continually accusing us and bringing condemnation upon us. While we cannot change the memory, we can change the lie embedded in the memory. The Cycle of Illumination looks like this:

Tree of Bondage vs. Tree of Freedom

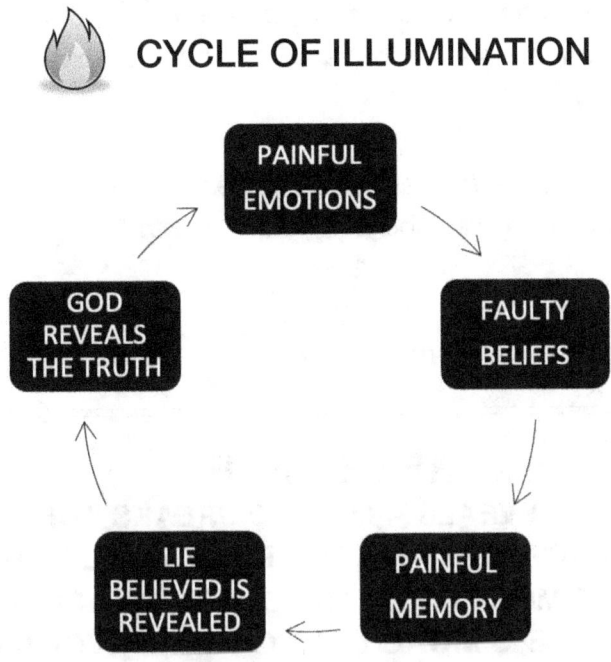

CYCLE OF ILLUMINATION

FIVE STEPS OF SHEDDING THE LIGHT:

1. Start with the immediate emotion. As the person to get in touch with the emotion they are feeling, and stay with it, don't run from it (e.g., Shame).

2. As them what that emotion tells them about themselves (e.g., I'm a failure).

3. Ask them to think about the first time they ever felt that way. This will usually take them back to a memory (e.g., Remembrance of being scolded for not doing something right).

4. Question: As an adult looking back on this, is it true that you were a failure? As an adult, they can now see that the judgment upon them at that time in relation to their age was not realistic. They realize they have believed a lie (often repeated over and over in their lifetime).

5. We ask the Lord to show them the truth. (e.g., The Lord will show them that people learn from their failure.) Sometimes God will reveal that the person scolding them was stressed by something else and will help them forgive those who were unreasonable in their judgment.

BIBLICAL REFLECTIONS:

I Corinthians 2:10-11 — *"But God hath revealed them unto us by his Spirit: for the Spirit searcheth all things, yea, the deep things of God For what man knoweth no man, save the spirit of man which is in him? Even so the things of God knoweth no man, but the Spirit of God."*

Psalms 139: 1-2— *"O Lord, thou hast searched me; and you know me. Thou knowest my down-sitting and my uprising, thou understandeth my thought afar off. Thou compassest my path and my lying down, and art acquainted with all my ways."*

I Corinthians 14:25— *"And THUS are the secrets of his heart made manifest. And so falling down on his face he will worship GOD, and report that God is in you of a truth."*

Hebrews 11:6— *"But without faith, it is impossible to please Him: for he that cometh to God must believe that He is, and that He is a rewarder of them that diligently seek him."*

REMEMBER....
EACH TIME GOD REVEALS A LIE AND SPEAKS THE TRUTH OVER IT,
THE LIE IS DISPELLED, AND THE EMOTIONAL PAIN IS HEALED.
IF MORE PAIN EXISTS, THAT IS A SIGN
THERE IS MORE THAN ONE LIE INVOLVED.
REPEAT THE STEPS
UNTIL ALL THE PAIN IS GONE
AND YOU HAVE
COMPLETE PEACE WITH IT.

REFLECTIVE EXERCISE: TREE OF BONDAGE & CYCLE OF ILLUMINATION

Identify the elements of the tree of bondage in Dan's life and the fruit that came from that bondage:
_____
_____

Identify why Dan felt un-empowered and depressed:
_____
_____

Identify the five steps of illumination:
_____
_____

Identify why our beliefs have such power over our lives:
_____
_____

Diagram your Cycle of Illumination:

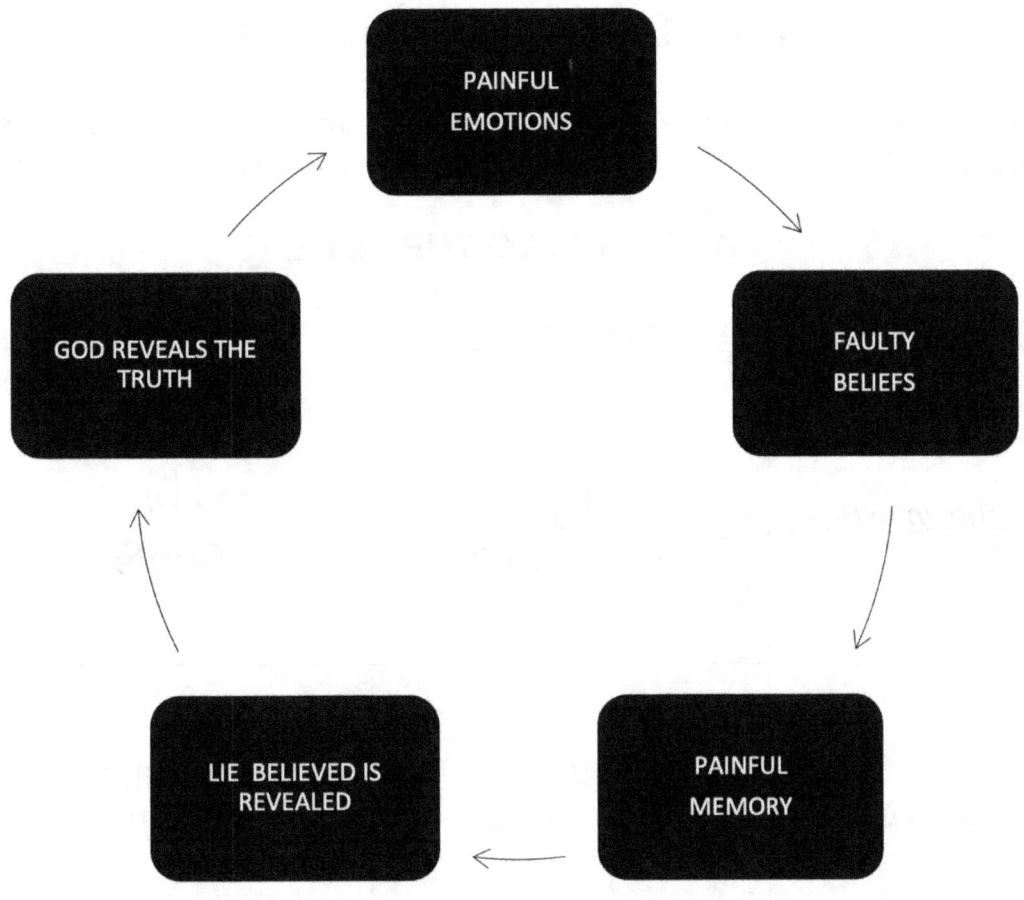

- Identify your emotion and trace it back to the memory...
- Identify the memory and allow the emotion to identify the belief surrounding that memory..........
- Identify the actions you took...how your body responded to this belief.....................
- As a child, you believed that belief to be true. Now, as an adult, reexamine that belief.
- Is that belief true based upon God's Word....the ultimate TRUTH????
- **IDENTIFY THE TRUTH ACCORDING TO GOD'S WORD**

Session Five

FROM DARKNESS TO LIGHT

"Search me, O God and know my heart: test me and know my thoughts, and see if there is any wicked way in me and lead me in the way everlasting." —Psalm 139:23-24

WINDOWS TO THE SOUL

	Known to Self	Unknown to Self
Known to Self	My Public Self	My Blind Spots
Unknown to Self	My Hidden Self	My Unconscious Self

JO-HARI WINDOW

The Jo-Hari Window, named for its creators—Joseph Luft and Harry Ingham, in 1955(1) *(www.communicationskills/johariwindow-model)—is a valuable tool that can help us understand how to live more effective lives. There are four "panes" on the Jo-Hari Window that represent four parts of our Self. Our Public Self is what we show others. Our Hidden Self is what we choose to hide. Our Blind Spots are the parts of us that others see but we do not. Our Unconscious Self is the part of us we do not see nor do others. We all have these four parts of Self, but their respective sizes vary in each of us.*

    A more <u>fully aware</u> person understands why he acts the way he does and is genuine towards others. He is in touch with his needs, feelings, and values—his *True Self* or identity. **A generally <u>unaware</u> person** doesn't understand why he does the things he does and has significant *Blind Spots*. He is often on guard and less genuine with others because he has a substantial *Hidden Self* as a defense against his own shame.

    When we have significant pain—usually from childhood—it can cause us to use whatever defenses we can to survive. They may help for a short time but can cause problems in the long run since we often need to detach from our feelings and our *True Self* and out of touch with who we really are.

Throughout this book, we will use several different tools and assessments to help us determine what our own Jo-Hari Window looks like at the present time as we try to discover our true selves. In this chapter we will begin to use the Jo-Hari Window as well as other tools to shed light into our lives and the lives of others in order to uncover root lies of the enemy that keep us locked in patterns that lead to death. The eight assessment tools listed below were specifically chosen for this course. They are:

1. GENOGRAM: A diagram of three generations of one's family history and family dynamics that provide a profile through which we can discern the roots or beginnings of certain dynamics. *(Best resource: Genograms in Family Assessment by Monica McGoldrick & Randy Gerson, Norton Publishing 1985) My material came from conference notes and handouts.*

2. PRAYER MINISTRY QUESTIONNAIRE: A questionnaire used by some Christian counselors or professionals to gather significant information about an individual's life history. It can provide insight into root causes or indicators of causes that may have contributed to our dysfunctional behaviors or illnesses. *(Adapted from Neil Anderson's material, Harvest House, 1993)*

3. DEVELOPMENTAL SCARS CHART: This is where we look at each developmental stage in our life to determine if or when any major events may have impacted it. Depending on the developmental stage we were in at the time, it can help to explain how it may have affected our adulthood. *(From Growing Up Again by Jean Illsley Clark and Connie Dawson, Hazelden Education, 1989)*

4. DEFENSE MECHANISMS: A way of determining the dysfunctional behaviors we use to protect ourselves. These behaviors often reflect our beliefs about the world and ourselves. *(Best reference: Protecting the Self: Defense Mechanisms in Action by Phoebe Cramer, PhD.)*

5. CYCLE OF SIN AND ADDICTION: A diagram that describes the cycle of thinking based on faulty beliefs that lead to survival defenses and behaviors that can become addictive in nature. *(From Out of the Shadows, Understanding Sexual Addiction by Patrick Carnes)*

6. FAMILY VALUES CHART: Assessing the makeup of a family and how it protects itself from the world in order to survive circumstances that could influence its health and well-being. *(Best reference is Bowen Family Systems Theory materials—My material came from my workshop notes from a training for Human Growth & Development, 1975–6)*

7. FAMILY TYPES: No two families are alike. While there are many combinations of types of families, studies show that there are basically four different, clearly defined patterns of family life in our society. *(Family Types came from conference notes 1980's) Best resource, Bowen Family Systems Theory, Peter Titelman, PhD. 1990*

GENERATIONAL SINS

> *"I am the Lord thy God, which brought thee out of the land of Egypt, from the house of bondage. Thou shalt not have any other gods before me. Thou shalt not make thee any graven image or any likeness of any thing that is in heaven above, or that is in the earth beneath, or that is in the waters beneath the earth Thou shalt not bow down thyself unto them nor serve them: for I the Lord your God am a jealous god, punishing the children for the sins of their fathers to the third and fourth generation of those that hate me, but showing love to a thousand generations of those who love me and keep my commandments."* **Deuteronomy 5: 7-10**

Genealogies have become very popular since the decade of the 1960's. Websites, books and all types of resources are available for us to discover who our ancestors were and to learn a bit of history of their lives. Frequently, we see generational traits and characteristics that get passed down through many generations. In this study, we are interested in the spiritual heritage of our ancestors.

When Moses brought the Israelites out of Egypt, God had a plan to bless them. They had been in captivity for 430 years as slaves in Egypt. Owning nothing and having no say in what happened to them, the Israelites were totally subservient to the Egyptians. Being powerless, they developed a very dependent nature, always looking to others to care for their needs. As they were set free, they were exhilarated. Moses led them into the desert away from their oppressive captors and began to re-civilize them.

No other people had seen God work in such a powerful way. God spoke to the Israelites out of the fire by night and the cloud by day. He took one nation out of another using testing, miraculous signs and wonders, a mighty hand and outstretched arm, and performing awesome deeds before their very eyes.

The Lord showed them these things so that they might know He was God. From heaven, God made them hear His voice in order to discipline them because he loved their forefathers and chose them as His people. The Lord drove out evil nations before them and brought His people into the land of their inheritance. His last act before sending them into the Promised Land was to give them standards for self-rule.

God knew that the Israelites would need guidelines for their lives. Knowing that Moses would not be going with them into the Promised Land, He gave Moses the Ten Commandments to guide their lives so all would go well with them and their children in the land He was giving them. The Israelites would need to look to God for direction since Moses would not be with them. These Ten Commandments are just as important as guidelines today as they were to the Israelites when Moses lead them through the wilderness centuries ago. According to God's Word we read:

> *"But when the Pharisees had heard that Jesus had put the Sadducees to silence, the Pharisees gathered together. Then one of them, which was a lawyer, asked him a question, tempting him and saying, Master, which is the great commandment in the law? Jesus said to him: 'Thou shalt Love the Lord thy God with all your heart and with all your soul and with all your mind.' This is the first and greatest commandment and the second is like it: 'Thou shalt Love thy neighbor as thyself.' On these two commandments hang all the Law and the Prophets."* **Matthew 22:34-40**

THE TEN COMMANDMENTS

Deuteronomy 5:6–21
(Also found in Exodus 20:1–17)

1. *"I am the Lord thy God, which brought thee out of the land of Egypt, from the house of bondage. Thou shalt have none other gods before me."*

2. *"You shalt not make thee any graven image or any likeness of anything that is in heaven above or on the earth beneath or in the waters below the earth. You shalt not bow down thyself to them nor serve them: for I the Lord thy God am a jealous God, visiting the iniquity of the fathers upon the children unto the third and fourth generation of them that hate me, or worship them; for I, the Lord your God, am a jealous God, punishing the children for the sin of the fathers to the third and fourth generation of those who hate me, and showing mercy unto thousands of them that hate me; and shewing mercy unto thousands of them that love me and keep my commandments."*

3. *"You shalt not take the name of the Lord thy God in vain: for the Lord will not hold him guiltless that taketh his name in vain.*

4. *"Remember the Sabbath, to keep it holy. Six days thou shalt labor and do all thy work, but the seventh day is a Sabbath to the Lord your God. On it you shalt not do any work, neither shalt you, nor your son or daughter, nor your manservant or maidservant, nor your ox, your donkey or any of your animals, nor the stranger within your gates, so that your manservant and maidservant may rest, as you do. Remember that you were slaves in Egypt and that the Lord your God brought you out of there with a mighty hand and an outstretched arm. Therefore, the Lord your God hath given you to observe the Sabbath day."*

5. *"Honor thy father and thy mother, as the Lord your God has commanded you, so that you may live long and that it may go well with you in the land the Lord your God is giving you."*

6. *"Thou shalt not murder."*

7. *"Thou shalt not commit adultery.*

8. *"Thou shalt not steal."*

9. *"Thou shalt not give false testimony against your neighbor."*

10. *"Thou shalt not covet thy neighbor's wife. Thou shalt not set your desire on your neighbor's house or land, his manservant or maidservant, his ox or donkey, or anything that belongs to your neighbor."*

BLESSINGS AND CURSES

For every infraction of the law of God there are consequences to pay. Our obedience to these laws given by God will bring blessings, but disobedience will bring curses. The Bible tells us in Deuteronomy 28 the types of blessings we will receive if we are obedient to His laws and the various curses that will be encountered when we are disobedient.

BLESSINGS	CURSES
Deuteronomy 28:1–15	Deuteronomy 28:15–68
Protection	Humiliation
Exaltation	Barrenness
Health	Unfruitfulness
Reproduction	Mental/Physical Sickness
Prosperity	Family Breakdown
Victory	Poverty
God's Favor	Defeat
Long Life	Oppression
	Failure
	God's Disfavor

As one examines their family history, we usually look for things that are significant in relation to leadership, roles in the community, wealth, occupations, nationalities, etc. Yet, the most important characteristic that gets passed down from generation to generation is the character of the person and how they related to the world around them. Those who walk in God's ways are usually benevolent in giving of their wealth as well as themselves. They will characterize the life of Christ and blessings will flow from their lineage. Others who choose to live in rebellion to God's laws, for whatever reason, will manifest broken lives and broken relationships. However, just as great men and women in the Bible sinned, because of their humble repentance and God's grace, God was able to use them in mighty ways.

God has a mighty plan for every person's life, and though we may mark our lives with sin, God is gracious and does not want to lose one from His family. As we examine our genealogies and families considering the Word of God, and use the tools of prayer and intercession, God can set us free from these bondages to our sins and to the sins of our ancestors.

The Genogram

Genograms in Family Assessment by Monica McGoldrick & Randy Gerson, Norton Publishing, ©1985 plus handouts (1)

> *"I have been reminded of your sincere faith, which first lived in your **grandmother**, Lois, and in your mother, Eunice, and, I am persuaded, now lives in you also."* ~**II Timothy 1:5**

The Genogram is an instrument developed through family systems research to help us get a picture or profile of our family in order to assess the type of family system we had and the inter-dynamics that made us who we are today. Studies have shown that the family has the greatest impact on our lives regarding how we see ourselves and our world.

God planned for the family to be the place where we as children received our foundational teachings. God gave Moses the following words for the Israelites,

> *"Hear, O Israel: The Lord your God, the Lord is one. Love the Lord you God with all you heart and with all you soul and with all your strength. These commandments that I give you today are to be upon your hearts. Impress them on your children. Talk about them when you sit at home and when you walk along the road, when you lie down and when you get up. Tie them as symbols on your hands and bind them on your foreheads. Write them on the door frames of your houses and on your gates."* ~**Deuteronomy 6:4–9**

Moses continues in Deuteronomy,

> *"The Lord commanded us to obey all these decrees and to fear the Lord our God, so that we might always proper and be kept alive, as is the case today. And if we are careful to obey all this law before the Lord our God, as he has commanded us that will be our righteousness."* ~**Deuteronomy 6:24–25**

In Proverbs we are told, *"Train a child in the way he should go and when he is old, he will not turn from it."* ~**Proverbs 22:6**

In Deuteronomy, God says, *"...I the Lord your God, am a jealous God, punishing the children for the sin of the fathers to the third and fourth generation of those who hate me, but showing compassion to a thousand generations of those who love me and keep my commandments."* ~**Deuteronomy 5:9–10**

We know that God sent his Son, Jesus Christ, to die for those sins, but we must apply what Christ supplied to our lives.

> *"...When we were children, we were in slavery under the basic principles of the world. But when the time had fully come, God sent his Son, born of a woman, born under law, to redeem those under law, that we might receive the full rights of sons. Because you are sons, God sent the Spirit of his Son into our hearts, the Spirit who calls out, 'Abba*

Father', so you are no longer a slave but a son: and since you are a son, God has made you also an heir." **~Galatians 4:3–7** Even though this is written for us, and is a promise for us, if we do not know and claim this promise for ourselves and for our families, the old oaths and vows of our ancestors will still apply to our lives.

HOW TO USE THE GENOGRAM

The Genogram is a way to identify those things in life that impacted our families. The family, through its attitudes, beliefs and ways of responding to life plus the ways those things are modeled for us, set the examples for us for how life is to be lived. As children, we may not question but we do learn from those around us. As we examine our families, we will want to look at the following things.

In order to look more closely at our families, two helpful tools may be used to assist with this important, valuable exercise. The <u>Personal Inventory Questionnaire</u> *(*see back of book) is useful as a probe into the past. Many people have forgotten some of the details of their growing up years—the questionnaire asks probing questions to help you remember things you may have forgotten over time. This tool is also quite useful for anyone in the helping profession who has been or could be helpful to you in this journey. It provides an overall picture of who you are and where you have come from in a relatively short amount of time.

By using this questionnaire, we can begin the process of filling in our Genogram, a tool used to identify patterns (positive and/or negative) that may have been passed down from generation to generation. As we examine our families, we will want to focus on the following:

1. Spiritual strongholds of the enemy in the family history (e.g., rebellion, lying, unfaithfulness, abuse, etc.

2. Family beliefs, rituals, roles, rules, and values

3. Sins passed down from generation to generation (e.g., alcoholism, sexual abuse, divorce, adultery)

4. Patterns of interaction within the family (e.g., men and women are segregated, strong dominating women and weak men, or strong dominating men and weak women; boys cherished, while girls are ignored; children can be seen but not heard)

5. Roots of bitterness hatred, revenge, stubbornness, unforgiveness

Looking for Root Causes of Problems

As we try to help others whose backgrounds are not known, it helps to look first at their family history. It is easier for them to talk about other family members than themselves and gives them time to develop a trust relationship with the helper. It also gives us as helpers an understanding of where that person has walked and can help us in establishing compassion and empathy for this seeker's journey.

In order to get to the root of the problems, it will be helpful to look at family dynamics surrounding the following types of problems:
- Birth and birth order
- Untimely or timely deaths, unusual cases (stillbirth, accident, suicide)
- Miscarriages, abortions, stillbirths, births out of wedlock
- Marriages/divorces
- Occupation of both parents and those of generations past
- Ethnic background
- Cultural heritage
- Socio-economic level
- Religious affiliation
- Education
- Roles (male/female, strengths/weaknesses)
- Beliefs
- Mottos (one message you always heard from your family)
- Values
- Relationship of family members (close, distant, cohesive, divisive)
- How love was expressed
- How anger was expressed
- How critical incidents were handled
- Communications regarding money, sex, children, alcohol/drugs, death, and religion
- Parenting Style
- Lifestyle

HOW TO USE THE INFORMATION THAT YOU FIND

Now that we have more information about our families, we will want to examine the impact of these things on the following generations. Much as you would be looking for clues to a crime, you will use your discernment to look for patterns that seem to flow through the family. e information will be used to help us in the following biblical steps of the healing process:

1. To guide us in severing unhealthy or sinful bonds from the past, even from the womb, that are affecting us today. **Ezekiel 18:19–29**

2. To examine and change faulty beliefs. **II Corinthians 10:3–5**

3. To identify unhealthy patterns of family interaction and replace them with ones prescribed by God's Word. **1Corinthians 13:11**

4. To bring repentance and forgiveness. **Acts 8:23**

5. To facilitate the process of dying to the old self and living in Christ. **Ephesians 4:14–15**

6. To shed the light of God's Word into the darkness. **I Corinthians 4:5**
   - Mottos (one message you always heard from your family)
   - Values
   - Relationship of family members (close, distant, cohesive, divisive)
   - How love was expressed
   - How anger was expressed
   - How critical incidents were handled
   - Communications regarding—money sex, children, alcohol/drugs

Social or Relational Issues

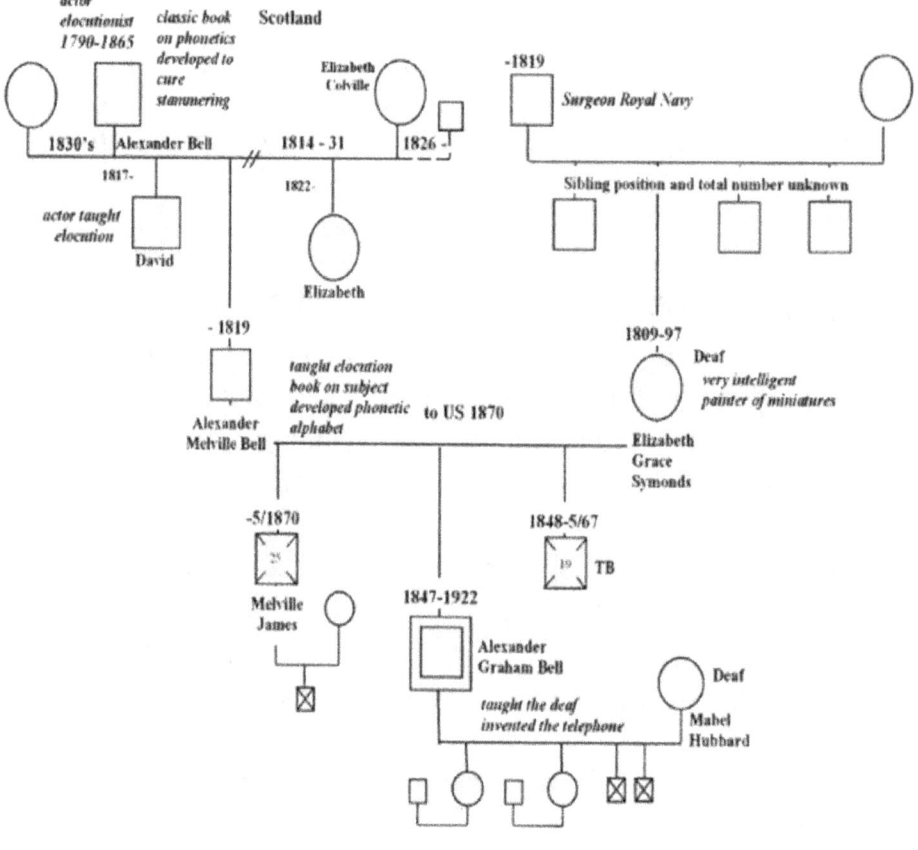

The diagram above provided courtesy of GENOGRAMS in Family Assessment by Monica McGoldrick and Randy Gerson., © 1985

GENOGRAM SYMBOLS

Diagram 2.1 Gender Symbols

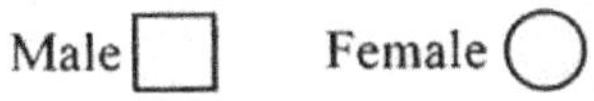

Male ☐   Female ◯

Diagram 2.2 Index person symbols

Male I. P. ▣   Female I.P. ⊙

Diagram 2.3 Birthdates and Deathdates

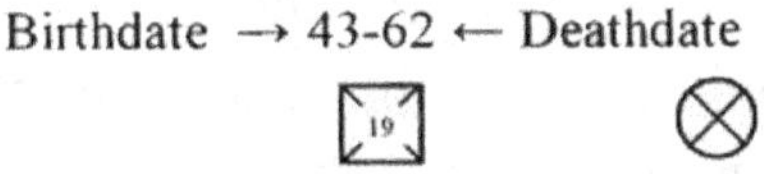

Birthdate → 43-62 ← Deathdate

Diagram 2.4 Symbols for pregnancy, miscarriage, abortion, and stillbirth

pregnancy △   stillbirth ⊠ or ⊗   spontaneous abortion ●   induced abortion ✗

Diagram 2.5 Marriage Connections

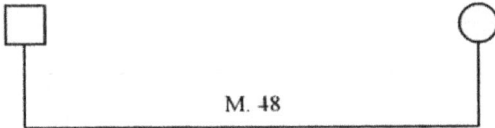

M. 48

Diagram 2.6 Separations and divorces

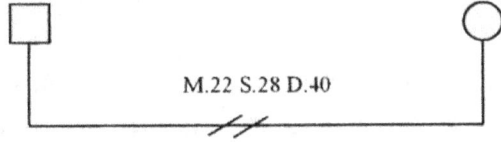

M.22 S.28 D.40

Diagram 2.7 A husband with several wives

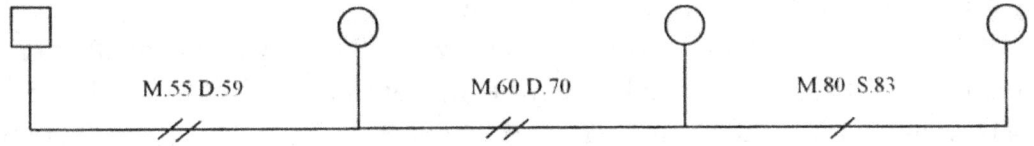

M.55 D.59   M.60 D.70   M.80 S.83

Genograms can be done online by going to www.genogramanalytics.com

REFLECTIVE EXERCISE

Reflect on three generations of your family beginning with yourself. Describe the personality and characteristics as well as significant things you remember about your siblings, parents and grandparents. It is just as significant to describe a person whether he has been absent or present in some way from the family. All these things must be noted (e.g., prison, mental hospital, divorced, etc.)

Identify the significant characteristics that you see in your dad's family and those things that characterize your mother's family.

- What roles did men/women/children play in your family?
- What problems seemed to "plague" your family?
- What were your family beliefs/values/mottos?
- Identify the patterns of interaction within the family (i.e., cohesive, conflicting, chaotic, democratic, etc.)
- Identify any roots of bitterness and how they seem to manifest themselves.
- What are the spiritual strongholds of the enemy in your family as a result of your family interactions (i.e., unforgiveness, anxiousness, vengefulness, alienation, etc.)?
- How do you see professions or jobs being repeated throughout your family history?
- What influence did your parents' heritage have on your life?
- How did your family's religious affiliation affect you and how do you see yourself?
- How was love expressed in your family? (men/women)
- How was anger expressed in your family? (men/women)
- Identify emotional defenses and toxic issues surrounding the following issues: (money, sex, parenting, children, alcohol).

NOTES: _____
_____
_____

PRAYER FOR BREAKING CURSES (Sample Prayer)

Father God,

You made a way for me to be brought out of bondage through the blood of Jesus Christ, my Savior. Father, you are a jealous God, visiting he iniquity of the fathers upon the third and fourth generations of those who hate you, but showing mercy to those who love you and keep your commandments. I am sorry for the sins of my ancestors and for their disobedience and rebellion against your commandments. They broke your heart and incurred your judgment.

I, too, Lord, have the same sinful nature and have walked in ways that satisfied me at the sake of losing my relationship with you. Father, I need you and your help, guidance, and direction that I may not be led astray again. I need the help of Your Holy Spirit. Fill me, Lord, that I may be empowered to resist the temptations to return to the sins of my father. I take the sword of the Word and cut the spiritual bonds of sin between me and my family and my ancestors. You have said that through our salvation, we are heirs to your Kingdom. I claim that inheritance for me and my family in the name of Jesus Christ, our living Savior. Amen

ROOTS OF BITTERNESS

Sin affects us spiritually, emotionally, physically, and relationally. We all have a basic need to survive. Though Elijah had destroyed all the evil prophets with his sword when his life was threatened by Jezebel, he was afraid and ran for his life. (See I Kings 19:1-14) He had had enough and prayed that he might die. However, Elijah felt no less the victor than his ancestors and fell asleep quite disgusted with himself. Even in victory, he was bitter and self-condemning. In his own eyes, Elijah was just a grasshopper compared to Jezebel's forces.

> *"Each Heart Knows Its Own Bitterness,*
> *And No One Else Can Share Its Joy"*
> *Proverbs 14:10*

In the story of the prodigal son, the older son reveals his bitterness towards everyone for rewarding his prodigal brother with a party. Attention was lavished on him when it was this prodigal brother who took everything, ran and squandered his inheritance. The older son was resentful that he had not been rewarded for all his years of faithful service. This bitterness blocked his ability to rejoice over his younger brother who was lost but was now found. The prodigal was the son who realized the error of his ways and humbly repented for his sin.

How rarely we find good will around us today. Angry drivers scream at each other in the streets. People fight to be first in line. Disgruntled employers and employees both demand their rights; but the common bond of God's people should be good will. Those with good will think the best of others and assume that others have good motives and intend to do what is right. When someone crosses us and we feel our blood "boil", how do we respond? We need to stop and ask ourselves, "How can I show this person good will?"

BIBLICAL REFLECTIONS:

Matthew 27: 3—*"When Judas, who had betrayed him, saw that Jesus was condemned, he was seized with remorse and returned the thirty silver coins to the chief priests and the elders."*

Genesis 4:1-8—*"Adam knew Eve his wife: and she conceived, and bare Cain, and said, I have gotten a man from the Lord. And she again bare his brother Abel. And Abel was a keeper of sheep, but Cain was a tiller of the ground. In the process of time Cain brought some of the fruits of the ground as an offering to the Lord. But Abel brought fat portions from some of the firstborn of his flock. The Lord looked with favor on Abel and his offering, but on Cain and his offering he did not look with favor. So, Cain was very wroth, and his countenance fallen. Then the Lord said to Cain, "Why is thy countenance fallen? Why is your face downcast? If thou doest well,, shalt thou not be accepted? And if thou doest not well, sin lieth at the door. And unto thee shall be his desire, and thou shalt rule over him. And Cain talked with Abel his brother: and it came to pass when they were in the field, that Cain rose up against Abel his brother, and slew him. it desires to have you, but you must master it." Now Cain said to his brother Abel, "Let's go out to the field." And while they were in the field, Cain attacked his brother Abel and killed him."*

Session Six

EQUIPPING GOD'S PEOPLE

"Therefore, be ye also ready: for in such an hour as ye think not, the Son of man cometh." —Matthew 24:44

OUR BROTHER'S KEEPER

"And of some have compassion, making a difference; And others save with fear, pulling them out of the fire: hating even the garment spotted by the flesh." —Jude:22–23

In the book, *The Coming Church Revolution: Empowering Leaders for the Future*, Carl. F. George (Fleming H. Revell, Publisher; Grand Rapids, MI, ©1994) compares the new church revolution to the process of the caterpillar becoming a butterfly. *Meta-Church* (*'meta'* being a Greek prefix used in the word metamorphosis) refers to the change in form that a caterpillar goes through on the way to becoming a butterfly. The Greek word metanoias describes the change in one's mind or thinking associated with repentance and conversion. Our minds and wills must "turn-about" so that we no longer hold stubbornly to our former ways, which block us from being fully obedient to God.

To make the changes necessary for the church to be victorious, we must realize that the church is in the world to be a change agent bringing the Light into a darkened world. Understanding and gave them power and authority over all devils, and to cure diseases. Authority is Christians is the key to power for Christians. T*hen Jesus called his Twelve disciples together, he gave them power and authority over all devils and to cure diseases. And he sent them out to preach the kingdom of God and to heal the sick.* —Luke 9:1–2

The whole realm of authority was challenged in the 1960's. Even the Word was challenged as the true Word of God. To bring order out of our chaos, we must again understand God's principles based upon His Word. When we take back our authority, the world will begin to see the Church in a whole new way. Without knowledge of God's Word, we cannot discern right from wrong. As we discipline ourselves in the Word and exercise the Holy Spirit, we will see the reality of Christ in the days ahead. Today there are too many Christians walking in lies and deception, thus, weakening the church at large. Our greatest fear is that we will upset someone with our beliefs. The anti-Christ spirit in our world today has challenged Christians to come forward. We will be further tested as we move into these coming days of ideological wars.

PRINCIPALITIES OVER FAMILIES AND NATIONS

"For our struggle is not against flesh and blood, but against the rulers, against the authorities, against the powers of this dark world and against spiritual forces of evil in the heavenly realm." —Ephesians 6:12

The enemy has many spirits that he sends out into the world to trap and trick humankind. God's people are not immune to these strategies. There are spirits assigned to families, communities, territories, and nations. The biblical model gives a description of people groups and how their actions and/or attitudes identified certain principalities that reigned over their lives.

> *"When the Lord your God brings you into the land wither thou goest to possess it, and hath cast out many nations before thee, the Hittites, and the Girgashites, and the Amorites, and the Canaanites, and the Perizzites, and the Hivites and the Jebusites, seven nations larger and mightier than thou and when the Lord your God shall deliver them before thee, thou shalt smite them, and utterly destroy them; thou shalt make no covenant with them nor show mercy unto them.*
>
> *Neither shalt thou make marriages with them; thy daughter thou shalt not give unto his son, nor his daughter shalt thou take unto thy son. Do not intermarry with them. Do not give your daughters to their sons or take their daughters for your sons, for they will turn your sons away from following me to serve other gods and the Lord's anger be kindled against you and quickly destroy thee suddenly.*
>
> *But thus shall ye deal with them: Destroy their altars, and break down their images, and cut down their groves, and burn their graven images with fire. For you are a people holy to the Lord your God. The Lord your God has chosen you out of all the peoples on the face of the earth to be his people, his treasured possession." —Deuteronomy 7:1-6*

Each of the nations mentioned had demonic spirits that characterized these groups of people:

Hivites: Were known for discrediting and slander; repeating matters outside of proper channels of authority and relations and tale bearing. (I Peter 4:15)

Perizites: Were known for division and contention, setting up ambushes to cause fighting against each other. (Matthew 12:25)

Jebusites: Were known for their filth, uncleanness, and sexual immorality. (II Peter 2:9–10, Romans 6:18–20, I Thessalonians 4:3–7)

Girgashites: Were a people known for anxiety and worry—a basic distrust of God and unbelief. (Hebrews 3:19) Their cares are choked because of their lack of trust in God. (Matthew 13:22)

Hittites: Were known for their discouragement, complaining, and murmuring which brings on depression and despondency. (Moses: Numbers 11:10–15); (Elijah: 1 Kings 19:1–9); (Disciples: John 6:58–60)

Canaanites: Were known for their superiority; making people feel inferior, paranoid, fearful, overwhelmed, intimidated and rejected. (Numbers 13:33)

Amorites: Were prideful, arrogant, self-centered, unteachable and delighted in finding defects in leadership. (Num. 21:13, Ps. 73: 6–9, Prov. 8:13, Prov. 16:18, Prov. 29:21).

(Author of this interpretation is inknown)

GROUP ACTIVITY: Meet in your small group and make note of how many of the above characteristics you recognize in your family, community, business, school, media, and persons around you. How do they influence your thinking and behavior? Discuss how the following characteristics of a warrior can help you overcome the influences of your culture:
- Confidence in knowing you belong to God
- Faith in God's Word
- Good conscience
- Steadfastness
- Earnestness
- Sobriety
- Endurance
- Self-Denial

THESE ARE THE DAYS OF EZEKIEL

"Then he said to me, "Prophesy to these bones and say to them, 'Dry bones, hear the word of the Lord'" —Ezekiel 37:4

When I read the account of the dry bones in Ezekiel 37, the Lord revealed a vision to me of dry bones in the desert for today and He stated, *"These are the days of Ezekiel."* As He began to move in my spirit, He told me *"This is my church. This is my Body—dried up and dead."* Then He showed me He wanted to breathe life back into those bones—the "bones" of His church.

The hand of the Lord was upon me, and he brought me out by the Spirit of the Lord and set me in the middle of a valley: it was full of bones. He led me back and forth among them, and I saw a great many bones on the floor of the valley, bones that were very dry. He asked me, 'Son of man, can these bones live?' I said, 'O Sovereign Lord, you alone know.' Then he said to me 'Prophesy to these bones and say to them, Dry bones, hear the word of the Lord! This is what the sovereign Lord says to these bones. I will make breath enter you, and you will come to life. I will attach tendons to you and make flesh come upon you and cover you with skin. I will put breath in you, and you will come to life. Then you will know that I am the Lord.' So, I prophesied as I was commanded. And as I was prophesying, there was a noise, a rattling sound, and the bones came together, bone to bone. I looked, and tendons and flesh appeared on them, and skins covered them, but there was no breath in them. Then he said to me, 'Prophesy to the breath, prophesy, son of man, and say to it. This is what the Sovereign Lord says, "Come from the four winds, O breath, and breathe into these slain, that they may live"' So, I prophesied as he commanded me, and breath entered them; they came to life and stood upon their feet—a vast army. —Ezekiel 37:1–10

Today, God is uniting us as a people. He is calling to His people. He is calling forth the bones. Denominations are coming together in one spirit. Jews and Christians, apostles, prophets, evangelists, pastors, musicians, intercessors, teachers, counselors, and healers are all being called by Him. God is breathing life into them, re-joining the Body of Christ, and uniting us in His Spirit. The muscles and sinew are the equipping for the building up of the body and the skin is God's protection. When we have submitted totally to His will and allowed Him to do the work in us, He will empower us by His Spirit to do all that He has called us to do. He will blow the trumpet. We will hear the trumpet call and will know it is time for us to move out as His army to conquer evil.

God is calling us—you and me—forth and is giving us His Spirit. We are the generation that is going to be lifted as the dry bones. He is equipping us, as this is our time of preparation. God needs us joined together, each one linked to the other parts for strength and wholeness, each one strong in the Word and power of the Holy Spirit, working together with one mind and heart. He is calling us today to heal and equip us; thus, making us His mighty army. We are in for a spiritual battle.

EQUIPPING FOR WARFARE

"But when he, the Spirit of Truth, comes, he will guide you into all truth. He will not speak on his own, but only on what he hears…" —John 16:13

1. RECEIVING THE HOLY SPIRIT

<u>The Holy Spirit is God</u>. He is the third person of the Trinity. In the beginning was God the Father, God the Son and God the Holy Spirit. The Holy Spirit is God. The Holy Spirit is omnipotent. He is all-powerful, almighty and has unlimited power. He is omnipresent, meaning He is always everywhere. We cannot escape from the presence of the Holy Spirit.

In the beginning God created the heavens and the earth. The earth was without form, and void, and darkness was on the face of the deep. And the Spirit of God moved upon the face of the waters. And God said, let there be light; and there was light…Then God said, Let us make man in our image, according to our likeness; let them have dominion over the fish of the sea, over the birds of the air, and over the cattle, over all the earth and over every creeping thing that creeps on the earth. —Gen. 1:1–3, 26

The Holy Spirit is the Comforter. In John 16:7, Jesus told His disciples that He would soon leave them to ascend back to His Father, but He would not leave them alone. He promised He would send someone else to be with them. Jesus called Him a comforter–the Holy Spirit. A comforter is one who comforts, covers, protects, listens, and tells us secrets from the heart of God the Father as He walks with us.

> *Become perfect. Be of good comfort, be of one mind, live in peace, and the God of love and peace will be with you …The grace of the Lord Jesus Christ, and the love of God, and the God of peace will be with you all.* —Cor. 13:11–14

The Holy Spirit Knows the Thoughts of God. The spirit within each of us is 'the real us.' As we look at the Holy Spirit and hear His voice, what we are seeing, and hearing is the very heart of God.

> *For whom among men knows the thoughts of a man except the man's spirit within him? In the same way no one knows the thoughts of God except the Spirit of God.*
> —I Corinthians 2:11–12

The Holy Spirit will glorify me: Jesus. The Holy Spirit glorifies Christ by declaring Him or making Him known to us. It is the work of the Holy Spirit to throw light on Jesus Christ who is the image of the invisible God. Christ is to be on center stage, which is the desire of both the Father and the Spirit.

> *He shall glorify Me for He shall receive of Mine and show it to you. All things that the Father has are Mine. Therefore, I said that He will take of Mine and declare it to you.*
> —John 16:14–15

The Holy Spirit Convicts of Sin. The Holy Spirit is the one who will convict us of our sin and our need of Jesus. The Holy Spirit is our conscience. He does not bring condemnation, but He does bring conviction. Condemnation pulls us down and offers no answer, but conviction points us in a different way and gives us a desire to repent.

> *And when He has come, He will reprove the world of sin, and of righteousness, and of judgment.* —John 16:8 (NKJV)

The Holy Spirit Teaches and Reminds Us. It is the Holy Spirit who reveals to us the true meaning or intent of God's word. He reveals the heart of the Father to us through the written word of God. He will bring back to our memory a certain passage of scripture at the correct time, just when we need it.

> *But the Comforter, the Holy Spirit, whom the Father will send in My name. He will teach you all things and bring to your remembrance all things that I have said to you.*
> —John 14:26 (NKJV)

<u>The Holy Spirit Will Speak Guidance to Us</u>. It is the Holy Spirit who will speak to and tell us the will of the Father. He is one with the Father and Jesus Christ, and in John 16:13, He says He will only tell us what He is told to tell us.

> *"However, when He, the Spirit of Truth, has come, He will guide you into all truth; for He will not speak of himself, but whatever He hears He will speak; and He will show you things to come."*

<u>The Holy Spirit Helps Us to Pray</u>. The Holy Spirit comes to "indwell" believers. He is the third person of the Trinity and abides in the hearts and souls of believers. When the Spirit of Truth comes, He will guide us into all Truth; for He shall not speak of Himself—He shall glorify God. Yes, the Holy Spirit can think, feel, choose, and act. The Holy Spirit is present in us to help us know how to pray; to provide us with truth, the Word of God, wisdom from God, and to reveal to us how to pray according to God's heart. He will show us God's heart for the person or situation for which we are praying. At times when we are praying, a thought or picture will come into our minds regarding the situation, or it may be a biblical example that will reveal a Biblical principle. If we follow the leading of the Holy Spirit, our prayers will be directed by God and will be empowered by His leading. There are other times when the Holy Spirit will give you the heart of God for that situation and you will find yourself weeping, or in travail. That is the Holy Spirit interceding on your behalf. Romans 8:26 states,

> *"Likewise, the Spirit also helps in our infirmities. For we do not know for what we should pray as we ought, but the Spirit Himself makes intercession for us with groaning which cannot be uttered."*

<u>The Holy Spirit Equips and Empowers Us with His Gifts</u>. God never tells us to do something without giving us the ability to do it. He empowers us with His gifts. In I Corinthians 12, we find all the gifts of the Spirit that are available to those who receive the Holy Spirit. There are different kinds of service, but the same Lord. There are different kinds of working, but the same God works all of them in all men. These are listed as wisdom, words of knowledge, faith, gifts of healing, miraculous powers, prophecy, discerning of spirits, speaking in tongues, and interpretation of tongues. The gifts are different from the offices spoken of in I Corinthians 12:27–30 where Paul explains that *"In the church, God has appointed first of all apostles, prophets, teachers, and workers of miracles."* Paul mentions the gifts of teaching, helps, and administration. In Romans 12:4–5, He emphasizes that we all have different gifts:

> *"Just as each of us has one body with many members, and these members do not all have the same office, so we being many, are one body in Christ, we who are many form one body, and each member belongs to all the others. We have different gifts, according to the grace given us."*

II Corinthians 1:21–22 reveals two gifts the Spirit gives to every believer; one is His "seal of ownership" and the other is "His Spirit in our hearts as a deposit, guaranteeing what is to come." The specific purpose of the gifts of the Holy Spirit is for the building up of the body of Christ. To build up means to bring together, to benefit, to gain strength, and to expand the body of Christ through the ministry of evangelism. We, as born-again disciples of Christ, are to actively welcome, expect and embrace them. In summary, the Holy Spirit does the following: calms, circumcises hearts, coexists, comforts, confirms, controls, convicts, creates, empowers, equips, guides, helps, listens, protects, reveals God's Word, seals us, teaches and is thus, the Giver of Gifts.

1. REFLECTIVE EXERCISES: *Receiving the Holy Spirit*

Identify the steps of personal spiritual preparation before entering the realm of inner healing and spiritual warfare. Recognize the ways God provided for the body of Christ to be empowered through the Holy Spirit to meet the needs of our brothers and sisters. Steps to Receiving the Holy Spirit For those who have been baptized but lack the power of the Holy Spirit, it may be that no one told you to look for the gifts or perhaps you have never had a teaching on the work of the Holy Spirit. Now is a good time to take the following steps to receive the full empowerment of the Holy Spirit of Jesus Christ.

If you have not taken the step of baptism or have not confirmed the vows your parents made on your behalf in infant baptism, you may want to be baptized by repenting of your sins and ask the Lord Jesus to come dwell in your heart and be the Lord of your life.

2. KNOW GOD'S WORD

Without the Word of God, we cannot face the trials and sufferings of life on this earth. As stated previously, the Word tells us in Ephesians 6:12, *"We wrestle not against flesh and blood, but against principalities, against powers, against the rulers of the darkness of this world, against spiritual wickedness in high places.*

Since the beginning of public education, parents began to trust the spiritual growth of their children to the schools and the church. With the Bible and prayer taken out of schools, many mothers and fathers have chosen to home school or send their children to Christian schools. With many parents both working, time for teaching faith and values in the home has become low on the priority list. Without the in-home training, children are subject to a constant diet of "tolerance" and "relativism" along the road that develops multi-culturalism, not necessarily unity.

> *The Word of God is to be our guide to a constructive, healthy, productive, successful life—a life that leads to righteousness and eternal life with God. It is a guide to keep us from destroying our lives.*
>
> *John 17:17—"Sanctify them through your truth: your word is truth."*
>
> *Luke 24:27—"And beginning at Moses and all the prophets, He explained to them what was said in all the scriptures concerning himself."*

> *Hebrews 1:1–3—"In the past God spoke to our forefathers through prophets at many times and in various ways, but in these last days he has spoken to us by his son, whom he appointed heir of all things, and through whom he made the universe. The Son is the radiance of God's glory, and the exact representation of his being, sustaining all things by his powerful word. After he had provided purification for his sins, he sat down at the right hand of the Majesty in heaven."*
>
> *Hebrews 4:12—"For the Word of God is quick and powerful, sharper than any double-edged sword, piercing even to the dividing soul and spirit, joints and marrow; it discerns the thoughts and attitudes of the heart."*

The Bible tells us *"My people are destroyed for lack of knowledge."* (Hosea 4:6) The Word of God is to be our guide to a constructive, healthy, productive, successful life—a life that leads to righteousness and eternal life with God. It is a guide to keep us from destroying our lives.

3. WEAR THE ARMOR OF GOD
Consider what the Word says in Ephesians 6:11–18:

> *Put on the full armor of God so that you can take your stand against the devil's schemes. For our struggle is not against flesh and blood, but against the rulers, against the authorities, against the powers of this dark world and against the spiritual forces of evil in the heavenly realms. Therefore, put on the full armor of God, so that when the day of evil comes, you may be able to stand your ground and after you have done everything, so stand firm then, with the belt of truth buckled around your waist, with the breastplate of righteousness in place and with your feet fitted with the readiness that comes from the gospel of peace. In addition to all this, take up the shield of faith, with which you would extinguish all the flaming arrows of the evil one. Take the helmet of salvation and the sword of the Spirit, which is the word of God. And pray in the Spirit on all occasions with all kinds of prayers and requests. Be alert and always keep on praying for all the saints."*
>
> **N**o Soldier Goes to Battle Without His Gear
> **N**o Christian Soldier Goes to Battle
> **W**ithout His Spiritual Armor

THE HELMET OF SALVATION
This piece of armor is designed to protect our minds and our attitudes towards those who are around us at any given time. When the tempter comes to us with evil insinuations against the grace of God, we need this helmet of salvation in order to keep our head on straight. The helmet of salvation ensures the trustworthiness of God's promises to us and His ability to save us to the utmost. We should not rush into battle without the helmet of salvation firmly fixed upon our heads. Our salvation is secure, and our redemption is glorious. Many of us who are caregivers become burned out because we try

to battle in the flesh. We must understand that if we are not saved, we cannot bring another person to salvation. No matter how much healing or deliverance a person receives, he cannot walk in the freedom that Christ has won for him if he has not accepted the gift of Christ. The person must accept and believe Christ to receive the strength and power of Christ in him who defeats the powers of evil.

Our minds are the playground of the enemy who loves to deceive and to lie to us. When we believe these lies, he can keep us so focused on protecting ourselves that we shut God out and everyone who wants to help us. He will have us believing lies that will destroy our relationships as well as our image of ourselves. When God's Word is written in our minds and we dwell on that, we are steadfast, having a guide and rudder as well as a map for our lives.

THE BREASTPLATE OF RIGHTEOUSNESS

It is with the breastplate of righteousness that we find clear and true protection. We ward off the attacks of the enemy when we understand that we are clothed with Christ's righteousness and not our own.

As we walk in the ways of God, we are protected by God's promises. Moses presents the Ten Commandments (See Deuteronomy 5) as the guide for living to God's people.

God wanted his people to be prosperous, happy, and healthy, so, as it says in Deuteronomy 5:33, He gave Moses these guidelines: *"Walk in all the way that the Lord your God has commanded you, so that you may live and prosper and prolong your days in the land that you will possess.* Additionally, in Deuteronomy 6:24–25, it states:

> *Let not sin therefore reign in your mortal body, that ye should obey it in the lusts thereof. Neither yield ye your members as instruments of unrighteousness unto sin: but yield yourselves unto God, as those that are alive from the dead, and your members as instruments of righteousness unto God. For sin shall not have dominion over you: for ye are not under the law, but under grace. Do not offer the parts of your body to sin, as instruments of wickedness, but rather offer yourselves to God, as those who have been brought from death to life; and offer the parts of your body to him as instruments of righteousness. Romans 6:12-13.*

We are to live as we have been called, doing right acts and right deeds in the sight of God. If we do this, our heart will not condemn us, and the enemy cannot condemn us. In other words, if our manner of life does not line up with our witness for Christ, then we will be found without a breastplate; thus, being vulnerable to the enemy. Just as it says in Isaiah 59:17, *"He put on righteousness as his breastplate, and an helmet of salvation upon his head; and he put on the garments of vengeance for clothing, and was clad...and wrapped himself in zeal as a cloak."*

> *Do not offer the parts of your body to sin, as instruments of wickedness, but rather offer yourselves to God, as those who have been brought from death to life; and offer the parts of your body to him as instruments of righteousness.* —Romans 6: 12–13

With some sensitive people, we think we must walk on eggshells in order to tell them the truth. We are afraid we will hurt their feelings. In other situations, we do not want to be honest with people whom we know are living in sin because they may get angry with us. We can see what they are doing and the price they are paying physically, mentally and emotionally; yet, we do not have the courage to tell them the truth. Thus, we cushion the truth with half-truths or color it with humor to stay on good terms with them and avoid confrontation. When doing this, we are not only giving them permission to be less than they can be but are actually enabling them to be deceivers. Hiding the truth also makes us deceivers. However, as caregivers, we must walk in truth.

> *When I say unto the wicked man, 'You will surely die;' and you do not warn him and speak out to dissuade him from his evil ways in order to save his life, that wicked man will die for his sins, and I will hold you accountable for his blood. But if you do warn the wicked man, and he does not turn from his wickedness or from his evil ways, he will die for his sin, but you will have saved yourself.' —Ezekiel 3:18–19*

> *"Kings take pleasure in honest lips; they value a man who speaks the truth."*
> *—Proverbs 16:13*

> *"I do not write to you because you do not know the truth, but because you do know it and because no lie comes from the truth." —1 John 2:21*

When a woman or young girl is encouraged to either willingly or unwillingly get an abortion, *who* helps her when she needs to confess? If we say, "That's okay, everybody's doing it," or "There was no other way," we are walking in agreement with a lie. She needs support in knowing the shame, guilt and grief she is feeling is because she has sinned. Something has been done that God stated would bring severe consequences. Repentance must be offered to her so that God's healing touch can be received through forgiveness and commit the aborted child's soul to the Lord for His keeping. Only then will she be free of the guilt and shame of her sin.

THE BELT OF TRUTH

We sometimes feel, with some sensitive people, that we must walk on eggshells in order to tell them the truth. We are afraid we'll hut their feelings. In other situations, we do not want to be honest with people whom we know are living in sin because they may get angry with us. We can see what they are doing, and see the price they are paying physically, mentally and emotionally but we do not have the courage to tell them the truth. So, we cushion the truth with half-truths, or color it with humor, to stay on good terms with them and avoid confrontation. When we do this, we are not only giving them permission to be less than they can be, but we are enabling them to be deceivers. Hiding the truth also makes us deceivers. However, if we are going to be care-givers, we must walk in truth.

> **Ezekiel; 3: 18–19** says, *When I say to a wicked person, You will surely die, and you do not warn them or speak out to dissuade them from their evil ways in order to save their life, that wicked person will die for their sin, and I will hold you accountable for their blood. But if you do warn the wicked person and they do not turn from their wickedness or from their evil ways, they will die for their sin; but you will have saved yourself.*

THE SHOES OF PEACE

When we walk in line with God's Word, and trust Him and His Word to be true, we have peace. Children who live in a home where they know they are loved and protected, have peace. Knowing we are God's children who are saved by His grace and protected by His covering, we can live in peace. The lies of the enemy, when believed, rob us of our peace. If experiencing fear or anxiety, we are not trusting in God's provision and protection.

A word found in Philippians 4:4–9 that has helped many people through tough situations can be divided into the following four steps:

1. *"Rejoice in the Lord always and I will say it again, Rejoice. Let your gentleness be evident to all men. The Lord is near."*

2. *"Do not be anxious about anything; but in everything by prayer and petition with thanksgiving, present your requests to God. And the peace of God, which transcends all understanding, will guard your hearts and minds in Christ Jesus."*

3. *"Finally, brethren, whatever is true, whatever is noble, whatever is right, whatever is pure, whatever is lovely, whatever is admirable, if anything is excellent or praiseworthy, think about such things."*

4. *"Whatever you have learned or received or heard from me, or seen in me, put into practice, and the God of peace will be with you."*

When following these steps, we will walk in the shoes of peace and rid ourselves of all manner of illnesses brought on by the body's reaction to disbelief, doubt, fear and lack of faith in an almighty God who loves us. The shoes of peace increase our mobility, enabling us to move quickly and fearlessly over unfamiliar ground because we know our security is in Him. When we walk in His Word and promises, we walk in peace.

THE SHIELD OF FAITH

Our faith is anchored in the person of Jesus Christ—who He is, what He has done and in nothing else. He is our shield. Many times, the enemy's form of attack will come as unbelief. We need to lift the shield of faith to resist the fiery darts of the enemy. The shield of faith will protect us from sudden, fierce, unexpected attacks that are the fiery darts. Perhaps these attacks will come in the form of depression, sickness, negative experiences, or questioning your faith. In II Chronicles, Jehoshaphat tells us to *"Have faith in the Lord your God and you will be upheld. Have faith in his prophets and you will be successful."*—II Chronicles 20:20

Daniel changed the heart of King Darius when his belief in God put him in the lion's den. Trusting God, Daniel entered the lion's den believing that his God was big enough to protect him, and God sent His angel to shut the mouths of the lions so that they did not hurt him. King Darius then issued a decree that all the people in his kingdom must fear and reverence the God of Daniel. (See Daniel 6:25–27)

The account of Shadrach, Meshach and Abednego as told in Daniel tells of their faith in God and His protection. When told that they would be thrown into a fiery furnace for praying to God, they replied—

Oh, Nebuchadnezzar, we do not need to defend ourselves before you in this matter. If we are thrown into the blazing furnace, the God we serve can save us from it, and he will rescue us from your hand, O king. But even if he does not, we want you to know, O king, that we will not serve your gods or worship the image of gold you have set up.
—Daniel 3:16–18

They were respectful, but honest, and when they were not consumed by the fire, the king ordered the whole kingdom to call upon their mighty God.

THE SWORD OF THE SPIRIT

The sword of the Spirit is the Word of God. In Hebrews we are told: *For the word of God is living and active. Sharper than any double-edged sword, it penetrates even to dividing soul and spirit, joints and marrow; it judges the thoughts and attitudes of the heart.*—Hebrews ``4:12 Jesus tells us in the book of Matthew, *"Do not suppose that I have come to bring peace, but a sword."* —Matt. 10:34.

Prayer for the Armor of God (Sample Prayer)

Dear Father,

I place upon myself the Helmet of Salvation as a reminder of my salvation and that I am a child of Yours, the King.

I place upon myself the Breastplate of Righteousness, which covers my sins and weaknesses and protects me from the attacks of the enemy that would condemn and deceive me.

I place upon myself the Belt of Truth that keeps me steadfast in your Word that empowers me and enlightens my path to protect me.

I place upon my feet the Shoes of Peace provided by Your grace. I rejoice that You order my steps and go before me. You are Jehovah Shalom, my peace in times of trouble.

I take up the Shield of Faith to protect me from the lies and deceptions of the enemy and the fiery darts intended to wound me and hinder my walk with You, God.

I take up the Sword of the Spirit which is the Word of God to use as my weapon against the enemy whose strategies are designed to be used against those who move in the power of the Holy Spirit. In Jesus Name, I give thanks for Your provision and protection. I delight in Your love for me. Amen

Session Seven

WEB OF LIES

"A false witness will not go unpunished as he that speaks forth lies will not go free." **Proverbs 19:5**

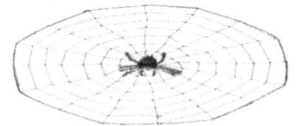

Sowing and Reaping

"Sow for yourselves righteousness, reap the fruit of unfailing love, and break up the unplowed ground; for it is time to seek the Lord until He comes and showers righteousness on you." **Hosea 10:12**

There is a biblical principle that underscores every act of man. Every word and every deed either reap good or evil. For every action, there is a reaction and a consequence, whether good or evil, based upon the motivation of the heart. Study the following scriptures to understand God's thorough plan. When He created the world, He set it up so that every function is interactive with its surrounding functions. Nothing stands alone in God's scheme of things. We learn this principle from Jesus,

BIBLICAL REFLECTIONS:

Job 4:8—"...Those who plow evil and those who sow trouble, reap it."

Psalm 126:5–6—"Those who sow in tears will reap with songs of joy. He who goes out weeping, carrying seed to sow, will return with songs of joy, carrying sheaves with him."

Hosea 8:7—"They sow the wind and reap the whirlwind…"

Hosea 10:13–14—"You have planted wickedness; you have reaped evil. You have eaten the fruit of deception. Because you have depended on your own strength and on your many warriors, the roar of battle will rise against your people so that all your fortresses will be devastated…'"

John 4:38—"I sent you to reap what you have not worked for. Others have done the hard work, and you have reaped the benefits of their labors."

Romans 6:22—"But now that you have been set free from sin and have become slaves to God, the benefit you reap leads to holiness, and the result is eternal life."

II Corinthians 9:6—*"Remember this—Whoever sows sparingly will also reap sparingly, and whoever sows generously will also reap generously."*

Galatians 6:7-9—*"Do not be deceived: God cannot be mocked. A man reaps what he sows the one who sows to please his sinful nature, from that nature will reap destruction; the one who sows to please the Spirit, from the Spirit will reap eternal life. Let us not become weary in doing good, for at the proper time we will reap a harvest if we do not give up."*

"The serpent ...said to the woman "Did God really say, 'You must not eat from any tree in the garden?'"
Genesis 3:1

Most of our unhappiness and emotional struggles began in the Garden of Eden. Eve believed the lie of the serpent and so did Adam. From that point on, their lives of peace and eternal life were over. We, like Adam and Eve, have believed the lies of the enemy. These lies are transported in many ways from person to person, through the media, television, radio, internet, newspapers, books, and C.D.'s, etc. Our mind may seem like a giant tape deck, constantly playing and re-playing the messages stored up in our memory, both lies and truth. The harmful ones produce emotional misery. Truth produces emotional health.

In his book, *Lies We Believe,* Dr. Chris Thurman explored for us the way we protect ourselves when we feel compromised or vulnerable in relationships. These come as naturally as breathing, because they, too, are a part of our self-preservation tactics designed right in our DNA that provides us with the ability to protect not only our physical selves with the fight/flight capabilities, but in every way our lives are threatened, the mind and body work together to provide protection of our heart and body. I have experienced in counseling that even after spiritual deliverance which we will talk about later, if people do not identify the lies they believe, but continue believing the lies or faulty perceptions that lead to their behavior and emotional problems, the problems continue to return...we will see from Dr. Thurman's studies that the lie is the issue ...or "demon"...so to speak, since it is the lies we believe that cause us to do what we do!

TYPES OF LIES WE BELIEVE
(Taken from The *Lies We Believe*, by Dr. Chris Thurman, Thomas Nelson, 2002)

1. Self-Lies
   I must be perfect.
   I must have everyone's love and approval.
   Confrontation brings pain.
   It is not safe to be honest about my thoughts and feelings.
   I can't be happy unless things go my way.
   No one cares about me; therefore, I must take care of myself.
   I'm unlovable, unworthy of love, unacceptable.

2. Worldly Lies
    You can have it all—and you can have it now (instant gratification)
    You are only as good as what you do.
    You can and should meet all my needs.
    You owe me.
    I shouldn't have to change.
    You should be like me.

3. Marital Lies
    If you'd change, our marriage will be perfect.
    If it takes hard work, we must not be right for each other.
    You can and should meet my needs.
    You owe me.
    I shouldn't have to change.
    You should be like me.

4. Distortion Lies
    This is more than I can handle.
    It's all my fault.
    If you're right, I must be wrong. If I'm right, you must be wrong.
    I'll never get through this. This is hopeless.
    This always happens to me.
    I'm a failure. I can never succeed.
    Nobody likes me. My life doesn't matter.

5. Religious Lies
    God's love must be earned.
    I can never be forgiven for the terrible things I've done.
    God hates me.
    Since I'm a Christian, God will keep me from pain and suffering.
    Death and suffering are bad and should never happen to anyone.
    It's my Christian duty to meet all the needs of others.
    A good Christian doesn't feel angry, anxious, or depressed.
    God can't use me unless I'm spiritually strong.

MEMORIES HOLD LIES

Our memories, whether good or bad, hold truth, but they may also hold lies. Looking back at our life, our memory of what really happened may be distorted or colored by our perception. An angry daddy may seem like a fierce bear to a tiny tot, when daddy just raised his voice. Nonetheless, fear struck at the heart of the little tot, and he gained fear of daddy. A mother who did not have time for her first child when a new baby came prematurely with many needs, may cause feelings of abandonment, fear or rejection in the older child. These memories may continually conjure up these feelings each time the child experiences the same type of activity. The spirit of fear, rejection or abandonment is now seeded in that memory and can be transferred to other types of events that simulate fear, rejection or abandonment.

There are guardian lies that keep us from remembering things we don't want to believe, for instance, every child wants to love and adore and believe in his or her parents. A child may not be able to face the truth of a parent being an alcoholic because of a guardian lie that "the kids will not have anything to do with me if I tell them my mommy is drunk all the time." This child can build up a whole fantasy about his life with mommy, deceiving himself of the truth. The lie can keep one from dealing with the truth that "mommy is an alcoholic". It is less painful, thus easier to believe that lie than the truth.

Victims of abuse, whether it is physical, verbal, sexual, psychological or emotional, have many lies. These lies are the roots of much pain, bitterness, unforgiveness, hatred, revenge, helplessness and hopelessness. We see the signs of abuse in the victims' physical demeanor and in their interaction with others as well as how they talk about themselves. The enemy is a liar, and most of his battles are strategic to destroying God's truth. In the book *Ishbane's Conspiracy* by Randy Alcorn, he identifies many strategies of Satan to deceive God's people. Listed below are a few of Satan's lies,

- Get them to give in to current trends, popular opinion and peer pressure, taking them right down the river of cultural conformity.
- Desensitize them through movies that make entertainment of horror, blood, violence and sex; especially let them see God's word mocked and ridiculed.
- Expose them to unrestrained sexual indulgence. Convince them that free sex leads to increased health, creativity, intelligence and inner peace, not confusion, depression, suicide, sexually transmitted diseases and death.
- Convince them they can live however they choose if they don't hurt anyone; that it beats Christianity with all those rules.
- Re-define the family. Take both parents out of the home by convincing them they need two incomes. Make single parenting normal. Let the television and the internet be the baby-sitter, keep them away from the family dinner table.
- Keep them busy, or use the phone, play station, and television to pull them away from family conversation.

In our lifetime, we accumulate many beliefs that are the enemy's way of weighing us down so we cannot move freely in the will of God. Many people are laden with lies that are such a burden they are always walking under a heavy load of guilt and shame.

BIBLICAL REFLECTIONS
I John 2:21 — *"…I do not write to you because you do not know the truth, but because you do know it and because no lie comes from the truth."*

Romans 1:25—*"They exchanged the truth of God for a lie and worshiped and served created things rather than the Creator..."*

Isaiah 28:15—*"...We have made a lie of our refuge and falsehood our hiding place..."*

Below is a chart of potential "Lies" which Dr. Thurman discovered many people believe and use to defend themselves against emotional and physical pain and suffering. All of us use defense mechanisms because that is part of the "fight-flight" reaction programmed into our DNA. Dr. Thurman has developed a Glossary of common defense mechanisms he found most people use...this is just a few of the hundreds that are used...especially when you consider people living in other countries with totally different circumstances. We still fall back on our defenses when we feel in danger or despair.

ACTIVITY: Each person will identify the defense mechanisms they use the most and write them on a piece of paper. We will begin to identify and discuss the ways we protect ourselves and the belief behind that action.

GLOSSARY: COMMON DEFENSE MECHANISMS
Developed by Dr. Chris Thurman, Psychologist, for his book *Lies We Believe*, ©2002 by Thomas Nelson

1. Alienating: Pushing other people away to avoid being confronted with reality.

2. Anger: A secondary feeling that is used to cover the primary (or true) feeling.

3. Attacking: Is usually a form of anger and the act of putting onto someone else or something else what belongs to you.

4. Being Obnoxious: A method used to push others away, or to manipulate them in order to avoid dealing with reality.

5. Being Reckless: A form of endangering self-and/or others to avoid dealing with the true problem.

6. Blaming: Not accepting responsibility or not putting responsibility where it belongs.

7. Changing Subject: A method of changing the focus to avoid the problem.

8. Cheating: Avoiding work, pain and/or responsibility; the act of *"looking for an easier and/or softer way"* of obtaining something.

9. Crying: Using tears to avoid dealing with the true problem or conflict. Also, can be used to get someone to back off.

10. Cussing: Foul language used to avoid the true issue.

11. Denial: Telling oneself it has not happened.

12. Destruction: Harmful tactics or methods used against an object, an animal or another person as an outlet for the true problem; a negative, angry way of acting out.

13. Excusing: Providing an alibi or a reason for behavior even when aware of the truth.

14. Explaining: The act of giving reasons for behavior to avoid self-responsibility. Behavior is irrational (justifying inappropriate behavior).

15. Flattery: Over-complimenting a person to get something in return.

16. Generalizing: Skirting the issue to avoid addressing specific aspects of a problem.

17. Getting High: Using alcohol or drugs to avoid or reject reality.

18. Hiding: A form of self-imposed isolation used to avoid self-responsibility by escaping the true situation, problem or conflict.

19. Hitting: A physical attack used to avoid self-responsibility for, or to divert attention from the true problem, conflict, or situation.

20. Hostility: A self-defense mode of anger/aggression used to protect oneself against a perceived threat.

21. Humor: Making light of or making a joke of something that is serious.

22. Ignoring: The refusal to recognize or acknowledge an existence or reality in order to avoid a problem, a situation or responsibility.

23. Intellectualizing: The use of scientific reasoning to justify behavior and to avoid responsibility. Use of lengthy argument or a small detail to distract from the task at hand. Attending to an issue or problem on a cognitive level to avoid "feeling" and emotional discomfort.

24. Isolating: The act of sealing off the outside world to avoid dealing with the truth, a problem or conflict.

25. Justifying: The act of giving reasons to make a "wrong" a "right" and to avoid self-responsibility.

26. Lying: Rejection of the whole truth or part of the truth in order to avoid self-responsibility.

27. Manipulating: Using coercion to have one's needs met instead of making a direct request.

28. Maximizing: The act of making something bigger or more important than it is. *"Blowing it out of proportion"* to gain sympathy or attention.

29. Minimizing: The act of making something smaller or less important than it is, usually to avoid embarrassment or punishment.

30. Not Listening: Tuning out by not acknowledging another person's message. Rejecting or avoiding the whole truth or part of the truth.

31. Passiveness: Withdrawal used to avoid self-responsibility in a situation or a conflict.

32. People Pleasing: The act of saying or doing what you think others want to hear or see. The goal in people pleasing is to get others to like you and to avoid self-responsibility.

33. Put-Downs: Derogatory comments to degrade another person so that you may avoid attending to what they are saying.

34. Rationalizing: Assuming that because *"A"* is true, and *"B"* is true, then *"C"* must also be true.

35. Resentment: The act of holding grudges avoiding responsibility for the true problem or feeling.

36. Running Away: Physically removing oneself from a conflict or problem in order to avoid confrontation or responsibility in dealing with the issue; used as a *"geographical"* cure.

37. Sarcasm: Saying the opposite of what you really mean either with anger or humor.

38. Self-Depreciation: The act of putting yourself down to avoid taking responsibility.

39. Self-Destruction: Threatening to, or endangering self in order to avoid the true problem.

40. Self-Pity: The act of feeling sorry for oneself as a way of avoiding self-responsibility and/or self-treatment, i.e., "If I'm hurt, sick, tired, busy, etc., then you can't expect me to do _____."

41. Sex: Sexual interaction used as a defense to avoid reality, or to change the way you are feeling.

42. Silent Treatment: Passive/aggressive behavior, which is used to avoid self-responsibility and punish the other person in order to convince them to take responsibility.

43. Smiling: A physical response used to cover the true feeling or response.

44. Squealing: Telling something about someone else in order to take the focus off yourself and put it onto someone else.

45. Stealing: An "easier, softer way" of getting what you want without taking the self-responsibility for the work needed to obtain it, or to avoid confrontation.

46. Story Telling: A form of explaining that hides the important facts of a situation or problem by using irrelevant information or statements.

47. Sulking: A form of withdrawal used to avoid self-responsibility and to draw attention to oneself.

48. Threatening: Attacking to get someone to back off a sensitive issue.

49. Vandalism: Destructive acts used to avoid dealing with the real situation or conflict.

50. Withdrawal: Removing oneself physically, mentally or emotionally from a situation, problem or conflict in order to avoid self-responsibility.

51. Yelling: Loud, aggressive, verbal attacking used to avoid dealing with the true problem or conflict; may be used to get someone to back away.

PERSONAL REFLECTIVE EXERCISE:
Identify the defense mechanisms you have used in your lifetime as well as the lie that laid behind it. Describe a situation in which you might have used this defense mechanism.
   What was the choice you made? What was the thought behind the choice?
   List defense mechanisms on a sticky note that will be placed on a cardboard brick…. symbolic of building walls using defense mechanisms.
   Consider how you built emotional walls to protect yourself from pain and shame.

Using a clean sheet of paper, draw your own <u>Cycle of Dysfunction</u> and identify your own defense mechanisms, thoughts, emotions, behavior and consequences. See if you can identify the original event through which the lie was seeded in your mind.

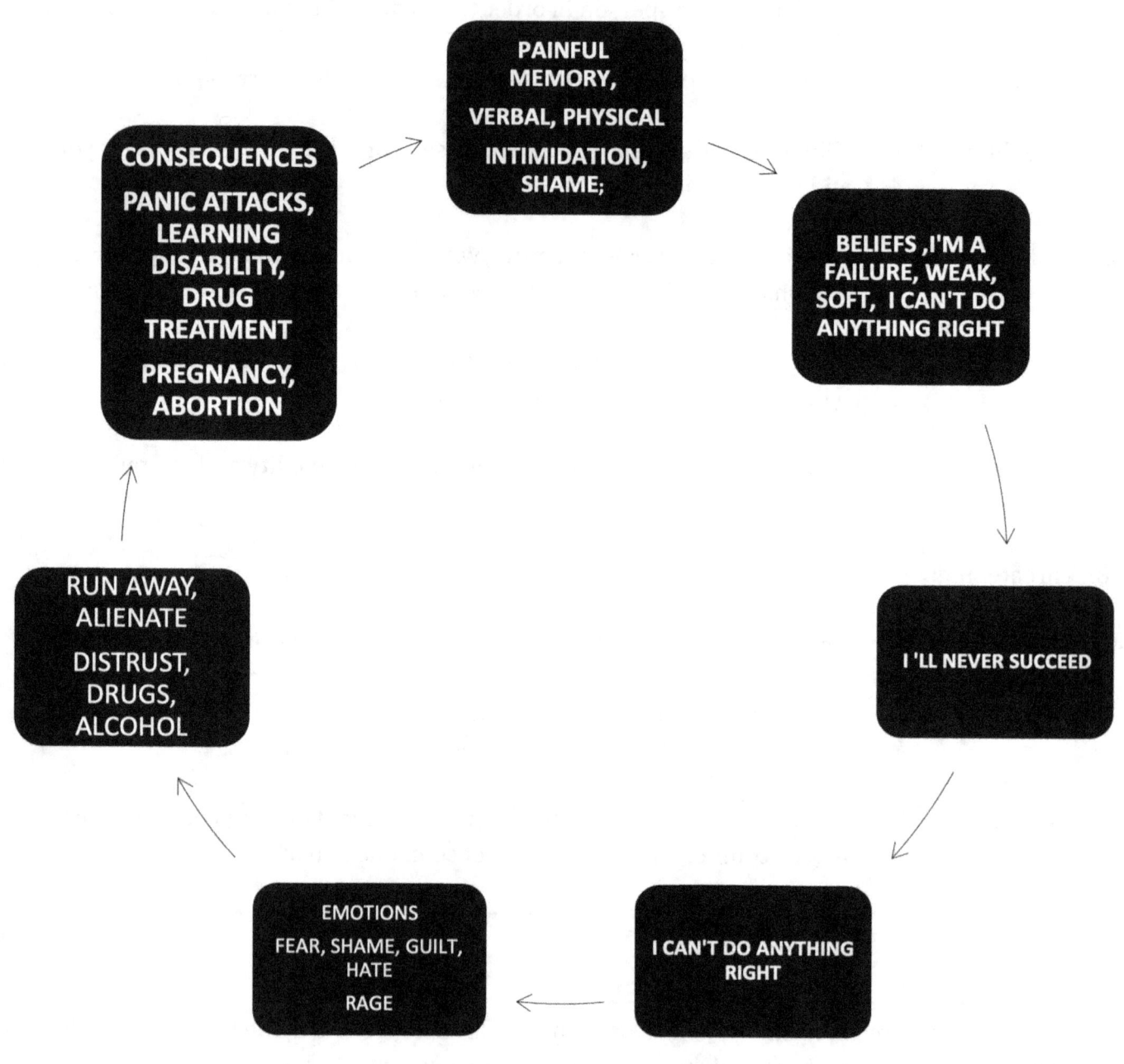

CYCLE OF DYSFUNCTION

"A man is slave to whatever has mastered him." — II Peter 2:19

The consequences of defensive behaviors are usually what bring a person to the counseling room. Typically, it is in the form of depression, marital issues, unfaithfulness, sexual issues, alcohol or drug issues, domestic violence, parent/child problems, familial problems, etc. Each problem involves more than the individual realizes, but the problems were manifested in his life because of what lay within.

As a person tells his story, listen for the faulty beliefs and identify how he responds. The reasons for coming for counsel are usually the consequence of his chosen responses to the faulty beliefs. By the end of the first session, we begin to identify for the client the cycle of sin and its consequences. Ask him to acknowledge this to be true or false. Begin to identify the wrong behavior and faulty beliefs and even trace them to the wound brought about by the person's perception of life's painful events.

A person can move from job to job, marriage to marriage, church to church, and still find himself repeating the same patterns of behavior. That is why it is called a cycle—people keep repeating the same mistakes, until someone helps them break it.

Cycles, if not broken, become addictive. The person finds one way to solve his problem, though dysfunctional, and is unable to look at another option. It is like being on a train on a track going round and round and nowhere to get off. Usually, by the time a person reaches the addictive stage, he cannot see any alternatives. This way has always seemed to work, that is, until the consequences catch up with them. God sends those who are not afraid to speak the truth and lend a helping hand to those who cannot break the cycle on their own.

> *Cycles, if not Broken, Become Addictive*

We may have only one opportunity to speak the truth in love to people. Understanding this cycle can be a wonderful tool to help us discern the cycle of sin and addition and to identify what needs to be done in order to correct the cycle in ourselves or others. Because of some of the defense mechanisms people have, the discernment may take longer than the first session, but the job of the caregiver is to be able to help people see what lies beneath the surface of their problems. (See Defense Mechanisms on pgs.77–99.)

CYCLE OF SIN AND ADDICTION

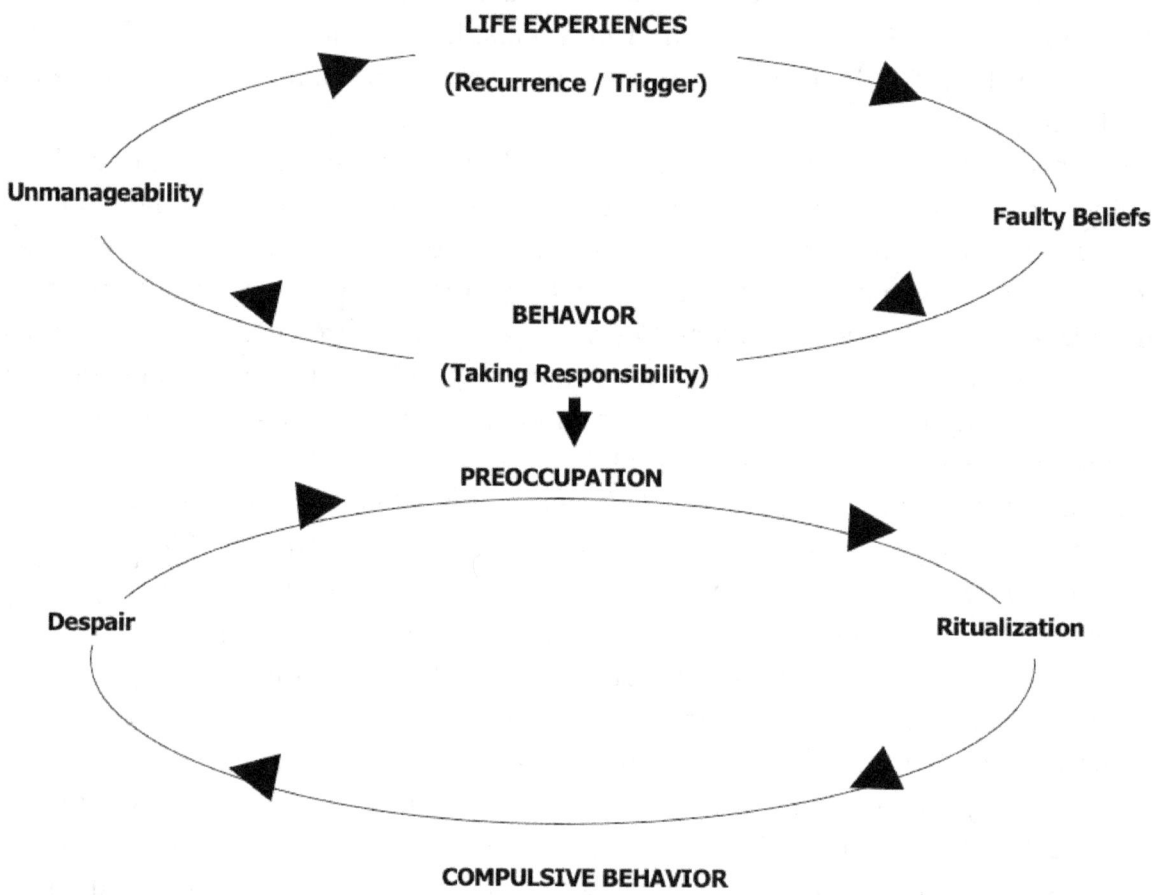

(Adapted from *Out of the Shadows, Understanding Sexual Addiction* by Patrick Cares, © 1994 Net Library, Inc. (2) See Appendix for listing.)

TOP CYCLE:

<u>Life Experience</u>—*Original Memories* (The accumulation of all life's experiences such as childhood abuse, first sexual experience, and any other event that influenced the person's perception of life).

<u>Faulty Beliefs</u>—*Original Lie* (a distorted view of self, others and life situations e.g., "I'm to blame"). When these memories are triggered, the sensory response is called the *Memory Echo*—it is the same as the original response and is a sign that the memory has not been healed and that the lie is still embedded in the memory.

<u>Behavior</u>—*The behaviors of choice when one assumes responsibility for 'fixing the problem.'* Because issues are unresolved, these choices are made from rebellion or the need to escape. The behaviors may be in the form of drugs, alcohol, work, gambling, pornography, food, spending, displays of anger, sleeping, health problems, etc. Choices become habits; habits become addictions. These can lead to impairment in more than one area of the individual's life. (See 'Defense Mechanisms)

Unmanageability—*The result of the addictive behavior.* Escaping to these habits and addictions usually impairs more than one area of an individual's life including: social, occupational, marital, spiritual, physical, educational, etc.

LOWER CYCLE—ADDICTIVE CYCLE

Preoccupation—*Compulsive fantasizing; intrusive thoughts.* The individual is focusing on the addiction ("I can't wait to do the addiction again). It controls them instead being in control of it.

Ritualization—*Routines that enhance the preoccupation with the addiction.* Habitual routines that facilitate the compulsive behavior.

Compulsivity—*Acting out of the preoccupation* (drugs, alcohol, sex, food, television, music, work, lying, and running). Repetitiveness. Can't get it off your mind until you do it.

Despair—*Feelings of guilt and hopelessness following the offense* (abuse, violence, drunkenness, rape, etc.).

BIBLICAL REFLECTIONS: Cycle of Sin and Addiction

<u>Hebrews 4:13</u> *"Nothing in all creation is hidden from God's sight. Everything is uncovered and laid bare before the eyes of Him to whom we must give account."*

<u>Psalm 33:18</u> *"The eyes of the Lord are on those who fear Him, on those whose hope is in His unfailing love."*

<u>Zechariah 8:16</u> *"These are the things you are to do:* **Speak** *the* **truth** *to each other and render true and sound judgment."*

> *If People Do Not Get Help in Breaking This Unhealthy and Dysfunctional Cycle,*
> *They Will Carry the Patterns they Have Developed Throughout Their Lives into Every Setting*
> *in Which They Find Themselves.*

Session Eight

THE FAMILY SYSTEMS MODEL

"Wives, submit to your husbands, as is fitting in the Lord. Husbands, love your wives and do not be harsh with them. Children, obey your parents in everything, for this pleases the Lord. Fathers, do not embitter your children, or they will become discouraged."
Colossians 3:18–21

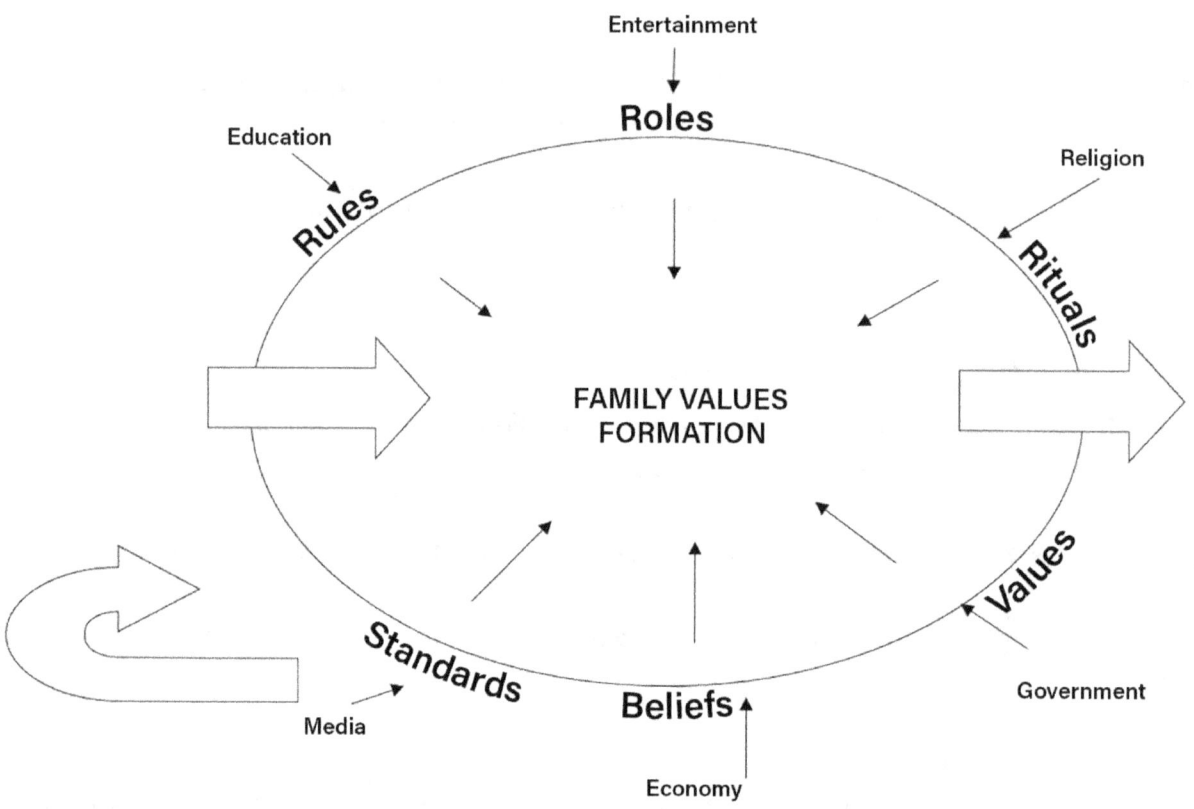

This diagram was from a drawing in my notes from a Personal Growth and Development class led by Proctor & Gamble Co. in the late 60's (best source: The Family Systems Model: American Psychiatrist Murray Bowen who began developing his **Family Systems Theory** in the mid 1950's). This diagram demonstrates the influence the family has on forming the choices we make as individuals. It also demonstrates the impact of information gathered from our culture: (schools, colleges, work, TV, Internet, newspaper and other media, books, church, government) These all put pressure on the family system which either strengthens or weakens the system and thereby affects the formation process.

The very formation of the family takes place at the point where two people come together in love to become one in marriage. Whether it is conscious or unconscious, both mates come together with hopes, dreams, values, roles, rules, and rituals in their hearts—hoping to create a family as good as or better than they had. They will take from the best they know and try to re-create that...or knowing the worst, try to do something different. In many cases, with unwed couples who are seeking love and healing for their own lives, they give no thought to the development of a marriage or family. They come together to try to fulfill a need in their own souls for what they didn't get from their families. We will look at an average couple and assume they have in mind the ongoing growth of their love through marriage and a family. They bring with them a certain picture in their minds of things they have learned in their lives that were meaningful to them, and will, whether consciously or unconsciously bring that about in their own marriage and family.

God gave specific directions to families as to what would bring about the best scenario to provide health, happiness and prosperity. We will look at several components that make up the healthy foundation of a family. As I look at the above Family Systems Chart, I see an egg. We all know what an egg looks like, and those who have cooked with eggs recognize that each egg has a protective shell that contains the egg white and egg yolk. We recognize that some shells are harder than others, and that the membrane lining the shell is stronger in some eggs than others. I see the eggshell as the pledge or commitment of the man and woman to unite as ONE body in taking on the responsibility of creating a family made up of the structure of the family as God intended; and the membrane as the beliefs, values, roles, rules, rituals and standards as that which creates the strength or weakness of the family unit.

ROLES

It is important for parents to set an example for children for what is truth and what is right according to God's Word. Children will repeat what they see and hear. They will see many examples of what is not good and right, but that which they see from day to day will mold and shape them into the persons of character you model and teach. Ephesians 4:29-32 and Ephesians 5:21-33 give us guidelines for our roles as husbands and wives. As we honor and respect one another and overcome our differences, in order to provide unity. As our children see us solving our problems and working through our differences, they will learn how to respect themselves and others.

SCRIPTURAL REFERENCES: Colossians 3:18-21, Ephesians 4:29-32, Ephesians 5:21-33

RULES

Parents are the child's first image of God. As we set things in order in our families, the child sees us as the person(s) who bring order, safety and security. Parental discipline in modern times has come under heavy scrutiny by others because of the misuse of correction and punishment. Discipline has also been unpopular especially if the parents are divorced and the children must divide their time between two parents. No one wants to be the one to discipline. Both are trying to be friends. Children need consistency and order to know what is acceptable and not acceptable. Changing rules from place to place, from time to time is confusing to children. They need structure and stability...not necessarily a place where they can get by with anything. Discipline should always allow for restoration. A child learns from instruction, but punishment brings shame and guilt and often rebellion. Hebrews 12:10-12 gives us a bit of wisdom regarding discipline.

> *"If anyone has caused grief, he has not so much grieved me as he has grieved all of you, to some extent—not to put it too severely. The punishment inflicted on him by the majority is sufficient for him. Now instead, you ought to forgive and comfort him, so that he*

> *will not be overwhelmed by excessive sorrow. I urge you, therefore, to reaffirm your love for him. The reason I wrote you was to see if you would stand the test and be obedient in everything. If you forgive anyone, I also forgive him. And what I have forgiven—if there was anything to forgive—I have forgiven in the sight of Christ for your sake, in order that Satan might not outwit us. For we are not unaware of his schemes."* (2 Cor. 2:5–11).

A child learns from instruction, but punishment brings shame and guilt and often rebellion. Hebrews 12:10–12 gives us a bit of wisdom regarding discipline.

> *"Our fathers disciplined us for a little while as they thought best; but God disciplines us for our good that we may share in his holiness. No discipline seems pleasant at the time, but painful. Later, however, it produces a harvest of righteousness and peace for those who have been trained by it." Hebrews 12: 10–12*

A parent's role is not to judge and punish, but to guide, teach and direct.

2 Corinthians 2:5–11 teaches us the importance of not inflicting punishment on a person who has made a mistake or did something wrong. These are times for teaching, not punishment. Paul urges us to reaffirm our love for the sinner. When this happens, the child will learn that he can move forward after a mistake. To punish and bring shame only causes a child to always be looking back at the pain and see himself as a bad person. This hinders a child's willingness to learn and move forward. The important lesson with mistakes is that we need to learn that we can grow wiser as we learn from them. Remember, many great inventions have been created through mistakes.

RITUALS

God ordained from the time of the creation, morning and night, light and dark. A time to lie down and a time to rise. A time to work, a time to play (see Ecclesiastes 3: 1–8). He designed man to work six days and rest the seventh day. Parents need to provide structure. He modeled a day for rest and worship, and times of celebration. God said," Man would work from sunrise till sundown, then rest." I heard a saying when I was a child that went like this; "Early to bed, early to rise, makes a man healthy, wealthy and wise!" We all need structure. Children need structure to feel safe and secure. Children need sleep to grow. Parents need time together. Children must learn that parents have a life of their own and need a time for personal lives; time to build and care for their own relationship.

Repetition teaches good habits like brushing your teeth, combing your hair, getting dressed and prepared for school, work, and church. It is ritual that sets an example that on the seventh day, we go to church and worship. It is ritual that sets a precedent for celebrating accomplishment whether it is a job well done or a birthday. Celebration is part of life and marks important occasions in our lives. That is why we as Christians celebrate Christmas, Easter, Pentecost, New Year's Day, Thanksgiving, etc. Each family needs its own special rituals like bedtime stories and sitting at the table to eat together. It gives the family opportunities to celebrate, bond and communicate.

STANDARDS

1 Timothy 3:4 says, "He (the husband) must manage his own family well and see that his children obey him with proper respect. (If anyone does not know how to manage his own family, how can he take care of God's church?")

In Deuteronomy 5, God reveals his Ten Commandments for the direction and safety of His people, the Israelites. In Deuteronomy 6:6-9, He said to His people:

"These commandments that I give you today shall be in your hearts. You shall Impress them on your children. Talk about them when you sit at home and when you walk along the road, when you lie down and when you get up. Tie them as symbols on your hands and bind them on your foreheads. Write them on the door frames of your houses and on your gates."

Do you set a standard for telling the truth even when a lie would get you more what you want? Do you set a standard for doing a job to the best of your ability? Do you set a standard for cleanliness, punctuality, politeness, kindness, settling conflicts peacefully? Without knowing it, our beliefs manifest in our behaviors and attitudes. We act upon our beliefs. And our beliefs are either what "seems good in our own eyes" or gleaned from the Word of God the Bible which is the guide God provided for his people. Jesus' words were full of guidance regarding how to live our lives. Hebrews 13:1 says,

"Keep on loving each other as brothers. Do not forget to entertain strangers for by so doing some people have entertained angels without knowing it. Remember you yourselves were suffering. Marriage should be honored by all, and the marriage be kept pure, for God will judge the adulterer and all the sexually immoral. Keep your lives free from the love of money and be content with what you have. Because God has said, 'Never will I forsake you.'"

BELIEFS

Christianity is not just a set of beliefs; it is a way of life and a community. It is a way of life taught through the Bible as well as the Torah. Biblical teachings have become the standards by which Christians judge right from wrong, good from evil. These guidelines or standards were set down by God through His chosen prophets and apostles throughout the early years of mankind. We have seen the strength of the American family weaken because of the cultural changes that have removed God's principles from our schools, churches, businesses, media, entertainment and government. Our education system has been drastically altered by rebellion against God's Word, as well as every aspect of American life. Parents, leaders and teachers are expected to be advocates for these standards. The Apostle's Creed is one standard that is accepted by most of the Christian denominations. These basic beliefs are:

- There is one God, the creator of the universe.
- He created mankind in His image.
- God is omnipresent, omnipotent and omniscient (present everywhere at one time, all-powerful, all knowing.)

- God is a person, Father to Jesus
- Jesus is God's only son who was conceived by the Holy Ghost, born of the Virgin Mary. He was crucified, dead, and buried. He descended to hell. On the third day he rose again from the dead and ascended to heaven and sits at the right hand of God, the Father almighty, from whence he shall come to judge the living and the dead.
- Children are a gift from God.
- Every life has a divine purpose.
- The Holy Spirit unites us with God. When we accept Jesus as our Lord and Savior, His Holy Spirit comes to abide in our hearts.
- We are all part of the "family of God."
- Forgiveness of sins is one of the key marks of Christianity.
- Christ died to seal our forgiveness by God and thus have eternal life.
- The immortality of the soul and the resurrection of the body.

VALUES

Values are demonstrated in the way we live our lives, how we spend our time, money and energy. Values are formed during three significant periods:

1. Imprint period from birth to 7 years of age.
2. Modeling period from 8–14.
3. Socialization period from 15–21 years.

In Deuteronomy 5: 6–21, God laid down His written law for His chosen people whom He had delivered from slavery in Egypt. He recognized His people had never had the freedom to rule themselves but had been oppressed by wicked rulers. These laws were designed to make his chosen nation healthy, just, and merciful. When the people followed these laws, they prospered.

These personal values provide an internal reference for what is good, beneficial, important, useful, beautiful, desirable, constructive, etc. Values generate behavior and help solve common human problems. Our values in life will determine our goals and destiny.

Over time the public expression of personal values, that groups of people find important in their day-to-day lives, lays the foundations of law, custom and tradition. Personal values in this way exist in relation to cultural values, either in agreement with or divergent from prevailing norms. A culture is a social system that shares a set of common values. These values permit social expectations and collective understandings of the good, beautiful, constructive, etc. Without normative personal values there would be no cultural reference against which to measure the virtue of individual values and culture identity would disintegrate.

Family Makes A Difference

"Husbands, love your wives, just as Christ loved the church and gave himself up for it. That He might sanctify it." ~**Ephesians 5:25**

*"Children obey your parents in the Lord, for this is right. "Honor your father and mother"— which is the first commandment with a promise—"that it may go well with you and that you may enjoy long life on the earth." ~****Ephesians 6:1–3**

No two families are alike. While there are many combinations of types of families, studies show that there are basically four different, clearly defined patterns of family life in our society. Look at the following family styles and see if you can identify yours.

THE FOUR BASIC TYPES OF FAMILIES

1. <u>AUTHORITARIAN</u>

    - The authoritarian family is one in which the mother and father take responsibility for the safety and security of the family. They assure that boundaries are in place to protect their children from accidents and injury.
    - They communicate love to each other and to their children, assuring them of their importance to the family.
    - The lines of authority are clearly identified and followed.
    - The rules are upheld by both parents so children know they cannot pit one parent against the other.
    - The family has rituals that bind them together (e.g., eating meals together, going to church, stories at bedtime, vacations, Easter egg hunts, birthday and anniversary celebrations, etc.).
    - The home is where children are taught how to make choices and evaluate those choices and their consequences.
    - Mistakes are seen as opportunities to learn.
    - Each person is treated with respect.
    - Godly discipline and instruction are used instead of condemnation and punishment when a child goes astray or uses poor judgment.

2. <u>CHAOTIC</u>

    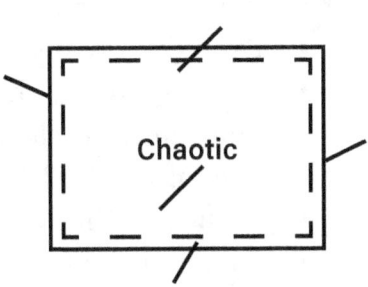

    - Neither parent is in charge.
    - Children are their own parents.
    - Children "pit" one parent against the other.
    - There are no boundaries and no rules, discipline, or guidance.
    - Everyone does his own thing.
    - There are no meals together. Everyone fends for himself.
    - Children and parents come and go with little concern for the other.
    - House is "falling down" around them: clutter, piles of dishes, repairs left undone.
    - Children are often confused and desperate for parents to make decisions.
    - Children often take over parental roles.

3. <u>RIGID</u>
    - The rigid family is usually alienated from the world.
    - They keep to themselves, prefer not to be seen or known.
    - A parent is usually dictatorial and accountable to no one.
    - A parent rules with an "iron fist."
    - Rules are very rigid, frequently unbending, and subject to the parent's interpretation.
    - Harsh punishment is meted out for any who disobey.
    - Those who are different are "outsiders."
    - What happens at home is "secret" and not revealed to "outsiders."
    - Punishment follows any "leaks."
    - Family "walks on eggshells" when Dad is home.
    - Family is manipulated by shame, guilt, demands, threats, lies, and abuse to keep them in line (including the spouse).
    - Family members feel weak and powerless.
    - Fear is the reigning force.

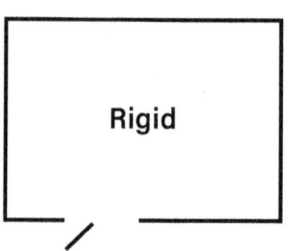

4. <u>SHOWCASE</u>

The showcase family will have all the appearances of a perfectly healthy family but on the inside, there is much insecurity about who they are and how they are to act.

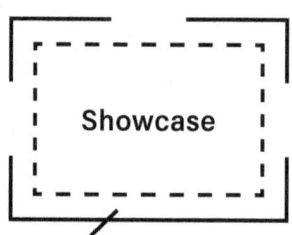

- Often their rules, roles, beliefs, and values are inconsistent because the parents are unsure of who they are.
- Often this is a family where parents have come from two different types of backgrounds; they know what they "should" be as a family but lack the unity to make it happen.
- Parents are insecure in their roles and vacillate between authoritative and rigid or chaotic.
- There is a lack of clear leadership.
- Rules are Inconsistent.
- Parents try to be friends with children rather than exercise parental authority.
- Parents often are highly responsible and active in church community.
- Punishment vacillates between harsh and acquiescent.
- Commitment is lacking to family rituals, traditions, vacations, and/or celebrations.
- Family has difficulty dealing with conflict.
- Communications are unclear.
- There is a fear of anger and conflict.

Transparency is healthy. When we are being transparent, it means we are being honest and pure of heart, with nothing to hide. When Adam and Eve sinned, they covered themselves with fig leaves, hoping God would not notice. We are the same way. When we are protecting "self," we show the world the characteristics we want the world to see in us but hide those things we do not want to be seen. When people feel safe and secure in their relationships, they will be transparent.

GOD'S PERCEPTION VS. MY PERCEPTION

My Perception	God's Perception	Scripture
I am unworthy/unacceptable.	I am worthy/accepted.	Romans 15:7; Psalm 139
I am alone.	I am never alone.	Hebrews 13:5 b Romans 8:38–39
I feel like a failure/inadequate.	I am adequate.	II Corinthians 3:5–6 Philippians 4:13
I have no confidence.	I have all the boldness/ confidence I need.	Proverbs 3:26; 14:26 Ephesians 3:12
I feel completely responsible for everything in my life.	God is responsible/ faithful to me.	Philippians 1:6; 2:13 II Thessalonians 3:3 Psalm 138:8
I am confused/think I am going crazy.	I have the mind of Christ.	I Corinthians 2:16 II Timothy 1:7
I am depressed/hopeless.	I have all the hope I need.	Romans 15:13 Psalm 16.11, 27:13, 31:24
I am not good enough/imperfect.	I am made perfect in Christ.	Hebrews 10:14 Colossians 2:13
There is nothing special about me.	I have been chosen/set apart by God.	Psalm 139 I Corinthians 1:30, 6:11 Ephesians 1:4 Hebrews 10:10, 14–18
I don't have enough.	I have no lack.	Philippians 4:19
I am fearful/anxious.	I am free from fear.	Psalm 34:4, II Timothy 1:7 I Peter 5; I John 4:18
I lack faith.	I have all the faith I need.	Psalm 37:23 Romans 12:3
I am a weak person.	I am strong in Christ.	Daniel 11:32; Psalm 37:34 Philippians 4
I am defeated.	I am victorious.	Romans 8:37 II Corinthians 2:14 I John 5:4
I am not very smart.	I have God's wisdom.	Proverbs 2:6–7 I Corinthians 1:30–31
I am in bondage.	I am free in Christ.	Psalm 32:7; John 8:36 II Corinthians 1:30
I am miserable.	I have God's comfort.	John 15:6, 16:7 II Corinthians 1:3–4
I have no one to take care of me.	I am protected/safe.	Psalm 32:7, John 15:9–17
I am unloved.	I am very loved.	John 15:9

Session Nine

BREAKING FREE

"I will free you from being slaves and I will redeem you with an outstretched arm and with mighty acts of judgment." —Exodus 6:6

GUIDE TO SPIRITUAL SURGERY

"Nevertheless, I will bring health and healing to it; I will heal my people and will let them enjoy abundant peace and truth." —Jeremiah 33:6

Just as a doctor does testing and examinations to understand a problem before determining what actions he will take, as a caregiver, we must be careful not to jump to quick conclusions about a problem. If we are dealing with a cut finger, it is not difficult to conclude that we need an antiseptic and a band-aid. However, for deeper cuts and wounds, we may need to take the injured person to an emergency room for stitches.

Similarly, the longer lasting and more persistent a psychological problem, the more research it may take to discover the root cause of the symptoms. First, it is important to identify the symptoms. The stated problem may be migraine headaches, depression, problems at work, or marital. In former times when towns were smaller and had intergenerational families, everyone knew our parents, grandparents, and every child. They knew everyone's family profile, character, and history. Pastors were at the same church for years so they, too, knew all about everyone in the family because they were there to baptize, marry and to bury generations of families and their relatives. A pastor could quickly determine the root of a problem. Today, however, when those resources are not available, and if a problem is deeply hidden, it may take other means to discern the root cause of the symptoms. In this book, we have shared tools that will help you get to the root lies you have believed because someone told you, or you perceived in your spirit because you really didn't know why you reacted the way you did. We have also found very informative questions such as our Personal Inventory Questionnaire, Spiritual Inventory Questionnaire or a Defense Mechanisms Chart such as are found in this book.

Once generational patterns and cycles that characterize the family have been identified, we look for underlying beliefs and issues that need to be addressed. In this section, we will address several necessary steps to take in order to receive total healing. It is most important to realize that any hope for healing will depend upon us and whether we use the power and authority given to us through our own relationship with Jesus Christ. There are several steps in the process of healing. The Lord will lead us through the process as we become ready spiritually. He will not give us more than we can handle.

Following, are steps provided by God through the shed blood of Jesus Christ through which all healing takes place. There is no formula and with some exceptions, it does not matter which comes first or last. Some steps would need to be in order. For instance, in order to know what to forgive, one must first confess; in order to know what to bind and loose, we must be aware of the strongholds and be ready to let go. Standing on God's promises is something we do throughout the process of sanctification. Deliverance takes place as we repent and forgive.

THE PROCESS OF SANCTIFICATION

The necessary steps include the following:

1. Renouncing ties to cults, occult, witchcraft and other cult or occult practices.

2. Renouncing all oaths, vows, and inner vows.

3. Severing unhealthy emotional, physical, sexual, and spiritual bonds.

4. Repentance of ways you have sinned.

5. Forgiveness of those who have hurt or offended us (even yourself);

6. Cleansing and purification.

7. Renewing of the mind, body and spirit.

8. Deliverance.

REFLECTIVE EXERCISES: *Guide to Spiritual Surgery*
Review your responses to the "tests" you have taken in previous chapters to prepare for your "surgery." What did you learn from your responses? Note your revelations below.
Can you identify your fruit as illustrated in the Tree of Bondage vs. Tree of Freedom?
_____
_____

What did you learn from your Genogram?
_____
_____

Can you identify a developmental stage in your life that would indicate a developmental scar? If so, what was the event and how did it affect you?
_____
_____

How would you diagram your addiction (if you have one)?
_____
_____

What, if anything, is hidden in your "iceberg?"
_____
_____

Which one of the four family types represents your family?
_____
_____

What lies have you believed?
_____
_____

REPENTANCE

*"In the past God overlooked such ignorance,
but now he commands all people everywhere to repent."* —Acts 17:30

Very few people understand the healing power of repentance today, because society has done away with sin. If we do not recognize our sin, we have no need to repent. We are told by non-believers there is no "right or wrong," that all is relative. Our sins are considered mistakes, diseases, genetic flaws, or dependent upon how one interprets the Word. Sin is acceptable—even *popular*!

Lying, according to a recent study by Josh McDowell (*Right from Wrong*, Word Publishing, 1994) makes us more popular. This could only be true in a truth-deprived society. The heart is deceitful above all things and beyond cure. According to the prophet Jeremiah, *"The heart is deceitful above all things and beyond cure. Who can understand it?"*—Jer. 17:9

We have been taught not to take sin seriously, everybody does it and there is no penalty to pay. Sin invades every part of our nature and personality—our minds, will, affection, conscience, disposition and imagination. Notice the list includes thoughts, words, and actions. This shows that, in God's sight, all sin is equally serious. Some of us think of sin as only serious acts such as murder, robbery, drugs, alcohol abuse, rape, etc., but the Bible "pulls no punches" and goes right to the point (root). If we hold on to hate, unforgiveness, rebellion, and disobedience, then we are holding sin in our heart.

Sin is… anything that fails to meet God's perfect standards. Anything we think, say or do that does not line up with God's will is missing the mark God has set for us to bring joy and prosperity to our lives. Those of us who do not know God, or His Word believe these sins are freedoms, rather than slavery, and don't even see the need to be set free from evil ways. We think that by receiving Jesus Christ as Savior and Lord of our lives, we are going to have to give up all our "freedoms."

Have you received Jesus Christ as your Savior? You can choose to live in sin and slavery and suffer the consequences of eternal separation from God, or you can receive Him and His salvation and be set free from the sin nature that rules you.

Even our defiance and unwillingness to accept His Word as truth is a sin. The Bible teaches that sin is lawlessness, deliberate rebellion against God's authority and law. No civil law forces us to lie, cheat, have impure thoughts, or sin in any other way. If we choose to sin, we choose to break God's holy law, and there are consequences to that.

BIBLICAL REFLECTIONS: *Repentance*

Ezekiel 18:32 *"For I take no pleasure in the death of anyone, declares the Sovereign Lord. Repent and live!"*

Jeremiah 15:19 *"Therefore this is what the Lord says: "If you repent, I will restore you that you may serve me; if you utter worthy, not worthless, words, you will be my spokesman. Let this people turn to you, but you must not turn to them.'"*

1 John 2:17 *"...The man who does the will of God lives forever."*

Revelation 3:19 *"Those whom I love I rebuke and discipline. So be earnest, and repent."*

REFLECTIVE EXERCISES: *Repentance*

You just learned that sin is anything that fails to meet God's perfect standards. Yes, also our defiance and unwillingness to accept His Word as truth is a sin. Review the Biblical Reflections listed above and understand how important repentance is to God.

Write your understanding of the repentance scriptures.
_____
_____

Look at your own life in light of these scriptures. For what sins do you feel the need for repentance? __
_____
_____

Go before the Lord and repent of your sins and make a new covenant with the Lord to walk in righteousness.

Prayer for Personal Repentance (Sample Prayer)

Father God,
I realize I am a sinner at heart and there is no way that I can be forgiven without repentance, a turning away from my sinful ways. I truly desire to be forgiven. Therefore, I repent of my sins(s) of (identify) and I ask your Holy Spirit to teach me your ways that I may not grieve you and your Holy Spirit. In Jesus Christ's name. Amen.

INNER VOWS—PROMISES WE MAKE WITH OURSELVES

"It is a trap for a man to dedicate something rashly and only later to consider his vows." —Proverbs 20:25

- The vows we make with ourselves become covenants, so to speak, with our inner self. Usually, these words are spoken at times when we are hurting and in pain. We have made these vows secretly; yes, promises made secretly only to ourselves. These decisions are seldom voiced aloud. For instance, if we have a painful fight with a very close friend, we may vow never to speak to that friend again. Or we may vow never to let anyone get close to us again. If we as a child have been particularly wounded by a female or male, we may make an inner vow never to trust persons of that sex again.
- Other examples of inner vows that we may make are:
  - I am never going to have children.
  - I will never tell the truth again.
  - I will not hurt people's feelings because they may reject me.
  - I will never get married.
  - I hate men; I will never let myself get close to a man again.
  - I will never let them know what I am thinking again.

There are other kinds of spoken words that bring curses on others. For instance, one example would be telling us that we are stupid and will never amount to anything. This statement becomes a curse over us.

God's Word tells us in Psalm 51:17 that He honors a broken and contrite heart, a heart that is full of compassion and teachable. A man is the measure of his word. If we do not keep our word, there can be no trust. Oaths are taken seriously by God and by man. A man who keeps his word is honored. Those of us who keep our word are recognized as people of integrity. Deuteronomy 29 shares an oath spoken over the Israelites who were renewing their covenant with God.

> *a Man Who Keeps His Word is Honored*

"You are standing here in order to enter into a covenant with the Lord your God, a covenant the Lord is making with you this day and sealing with an oath, to confirm you this day as his people, that he may be your God as He promised you and as He swore to your fathers, Abraham, Isaac and Jacob." —Deuteronomy 29:12–13

The Merriam-Webster Dictionary defines an oath as:

1. A solemn appeal to God to a witness of a promise.
2. An irreverent or careless use of a sacred name.
3. A vow as a solemn promise or assertion; especially one by which a person binds himself to an act, service, or condition.

There are times, however, in which we enter a covenant without thinking of its seriousness, and this can cause problems for us. We think we are the only ones who know about these oaths, but God is aware of every oath we have taken, and He holds us accountable.

Biblical Reflections: *Inner Vows—Promises We Make with Ourselves*
Job 22:27 *"You will pray to him, and he will hear you, and you will fulfill your vows."*

Psalm 51:6 *"Surely you desire truth in the inner parts; you teach me wisdom in the inmost place."*

Isaiah 19:21 *"They will make vows to the Lord and keep them."*

FORGIVENESS

*"Blessed is he whose transgressions are forgiven, whose sins are covered.
Blessed is the man whose sin the Lord does not count against him
and in whose spirit is no deceit."* —Psalm 32:1–2

Today, seeking forgiveness from God is rarely mentioned, yet every sin grieves the heart of God. We are told in Isaiah 63:10: *"… they rebelled and grieved His Holy Spirit. So, He turned and became their enemy and He Himself fought against them."*

Sometimes our own sin brings upon us the wrath of God. Yet for those of us who repent and seek forgiveness, He is quick to forgive. In our culture, forgiveness is man to man, but every sin against man is a sin against God and must be brought to the throne of Grace to receive God's forgiveness.

John tells us if we forgive, we will be forgiven. *"If you forgive anyone his sins, they are forgiven; if you do not forgive them, they are not forgiven."* —John 20:23

If we hold unforgiveness, it will block our blessings from God. Forgiveness is a powerful thing. Our unforgiveness can keep another person in bondage to us. Any relationship that is broken keeps people in bondage to one another until such time as forgiveness takes place. The state of unforgiveness allows the spirit of strife, revenge, resentment, hate, and many other spirits to abide in us. This also hinders the healing in the other person because it does not allow the woundedness in the other person to heal. The person we are angry with may not even be aware of our anger. There are times God will use one person to bring healing to many people just through repentance and forgiveness.

Forgiveness is a powerful thing.
    Forgiveness is a choice.
        Forgiving does not necessarily mean that we are going to forget.
            Forgiving is not pretending that the offense did not matter.
                Forgiving does not necessarily mean the person is entirely off the hook.
                    UNFORGIVENESS in your heart is committing emotional suicide.

STEPS OF FORGIVENESS: *Total Forgiveness* by R. T. Kendall, Charisma House ©2002(1)

1. Line your will up with God's will. Purpose in your heart to work the process through—regardless of the pain and fear.

2. Ask the Holy Spirit to shed His light into your soul to reveal the roots of the bitterness in your heart.

3. Be specific about what it is you need to forgive.

4. Identify your response to the offense.

5. Be honest before God regarding how you feel about the person or the event.

6. Forgive the offense.

7. Pray and ask God to forgive you for holding the unforgiveness in your heart.

8. Identify any inner vows you have made regarding your offender and renounce them.

9. Renew your mind with the Word of God.

10. Forgive yourself for your part and pray for healing.

11. Identify any area in which you are blaming God.

12. Release God, others and yourself from any false or unrealistic expectations you may have had for them.

13. Forgive God. Ask Him to show you what He was trying to work into your spirit.

14. Prayer for the person you have forgiven.

BIBLICAL REFLECTIONS: *Forgiveness*

Psalm 32:2 *"Blessed is he whose transgressions are forgiven, whose sins are covered. Blessed the man whose sin the Lord does not count against him and in whose spirit is no deceit."*

Luke 23:34 *"Jesus said, 'Father, forgive them, for they do know what they are doing...'"*

Romans 5:8 *"But God demonstrates his own love for us in this: While we were still sinners, Christ died for us."*

Ephesians 4:31–32 *"Get rid of all bitterness, rage and anger, brawling and slander, along with every form of malice. Be kind and compassionate to one another, forgiving each other, just as in Christ God forgive you."*

Colossians 3:13 *"Bear with each other and forgive whatever grievances you may have against one another. Forgive as the Lord forgave you."*

REFLECTIVE EXERCISES: *Forgiveness*
Take personal time with God and lift these persons in prayer to release them from the power of your unforgiveness and releasing them to God for His justice to be done.

_____
_____

Prayer of Forgiveness (Sample Prayer)

Dear God,

I know I have sinned against (name) for offending him/her (or holding unforgiveness towards him for his/her offense towards me). I am having a hard time forgiving them because it still hurts. Your Word tells me I won't be forgiven unless I forgive others. I know I have sinned and fall short of Your glory. Please forgive me for my offense against them. I was angry/bitter regarding (what angered you). Though I knew it was wrong, I allowed this to grow in my heart, bringing separation from my brother/sister as well as from You.

Father, speak Your truth to me and renew my mind with Your Word. I don't want to harbor bitterness/revenge anymore, nor do I want to blame others. With your help, I take full responsibility for changing this situation.

Forgive me, God, and release (name) from the unrealistic expectation I have had for them. I also release myself from all unrealistic expectations I have had for myself. I pray for your Holy Spirit to intercede to break every stronghold of bitterness and strife between us, and I renounce every lie the enemy has told me. I choose to believe that You can bring good from this situation. I place my anger/bitterness in Your hands and trust You to bring justice and peace where I have failed.

Thank you, Father, for sending Jesus to make it possible for me to be released from this heavy burden. Amen

CYCLE OF ILLUMINATION

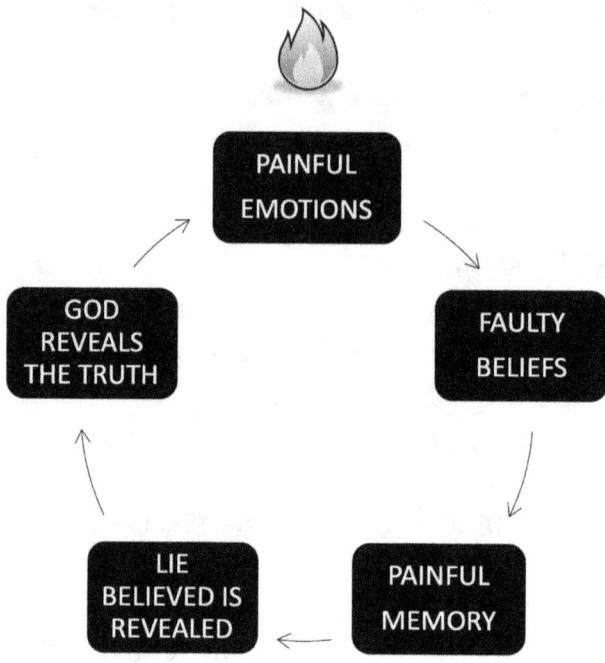

BIBLICAL REFLECTIONS: *Shedding Light into the Darkness*
Job 28:11 *"He searches the sources of the river and brings hidden things to light."*

Psalm 139:1–3 *"O Lord, you have searched me and you know me. You know when I sit and when I rise; you perceive my thoughts from afar. You discern my going out and my lying down; you are familiar with all my ways."*

REFLECTIVE EXERCISES: *Shedding Light into the Darkness*
As we learn to shed the light of God's Word and allow the Holy Spirit to show us what is in our soul, we will experience revelation knowledge that will identify the root of our pain. As we uncover the lies of the enemy rooted in the memory, we will experience freedom from the pain.

   Study the Biblical Reflections in the preceding section and be amazed at how God provides His Truth to uncover the lies of the enemy and set us free! What lie(s) is God showing you that you need to uncover to be set free?

CLOSING EXERCISE: *Dying to Self*
- Read Isaiah 61: 1-3—the call upon caregivers
    - Have students identify sins or lies they are ready to lay down at the foot of
    - the cross.
    - Give students the cardboard bricks on which they have written the lie/belief they are ready to give up to the Lord.

- Have them bring the brick forward as a reminder that they have laid their sins at the foot of the cross.
- Have each one publicly confess the sin/lie and ask for forgiveness, then lay the brick down forming a pathway to the cross (have a large cross at the foot of that which will become a pathway upon which they lay their brick).

- After students lay brick at the foot of the cross, give them their Certificate of Completion.
- You may serve communion by serving the bread and grape juice in remembrance of what Christ did for us on the cross. You may use Matthew 26:26-28 as the scripture
- You may also use this exercise as a time to encourage, give a certificate of completion for the class.
- Closing Prayer and affirmation of forgiveness

BOOKS WRITTEN BY MILLIE McCARTY, M.A., LPCC

HEALING THE HEART: Getting to the Root of Abuse, PTSD and Trauma

Developed in 2014 for The Healing Hub at the Gate for use in taking this curriculum to the nations. This curriculum is a composite of both books developed by founder, Millie McCarty, M.A., LPCC-S; *Pathways to Hope and Healing* and *Why We Can't "Just Get Over It" In* order to bring the core teachings of IIAC's ministry, we have chosen the most important sections of these two books. To receive the total benefit possible in healing ministry, the original books must also be read in their entirety. Revised, 2018

PATHWAYS TO HOPE AND HEALING—Getting to the Root of it All

by Millie McCarty M.A. LPCC

Copyright © 2002 by Millie McCarty

All rights reserved. No part of this publication may be reproduced, transmitted in any form or stored in a retrieval system without prior written permission of author, except in the case of brief quotations embodied in articles and previews.

Revised 2010—Edited by Cindy Johnston

Revised 2013—Edited by Millie McCarty

Cover photo and design—Lisa Hilty

Published by Ambris Publishing Co., Dayton, Ohio—ISBN: #1-929643-10-1

All Scripture quotations, unless otherwise indicated, are taken from *The Holy Bible: New International Version* (NIV)

Copyright © 1973, 1978, 1984 by The International Bible Society. All rights reserved.

WHY WE CAN'T "JUST GET OVER IT": Healing the Lasting Effect of Prolonged Stress and Trauma

© Copyright 2009 Millie McCarty, Author

All rights reserved including the right of reproduction in whole or part in any form.

Edited by Beverly Jo Garrison

First revision edited by Cindy Johnston 2012

Cover photo and design by Lisa Hilty

Published by Ambris Publishing Co., Dayton, Ohio—ISBN# 1-929634-11-x

Printed in the United States of America—Jan. 2010

All rights reserved. No part of this publication may be reproduced in any manner without written permission of author in advance, except in the case of brief quotations embodied in articles and reviews or charts that are public domain.

All scripture quotations in this publication are from The Holy Bible, New King James Version, New Spirit Filled Life Bible, Copyright 2002 published by THOMAS NELSON BIBLES, unless otherwise specified.

RUTH: SECRETS OF THE SILENCED VOICES—A Guide to Working with People with Dissociative Identity Disorders

© Copyright 2012 Millie McCarty, M.A., LPPC

Requests for information should be addressed to The Healing Hub at The Gate Pickerington, Ohio 43147, (milliehealinghub4u@gmail.com).

BIBLIOGRAPHY

Alcorn, Randy, et. al. *The Ishbane Conspiracy.* Multnomah Books, 2002.

Alcorn, Randy. *HEAVEN.* Wheaton, IL. Tyndale, 2004.

Allender, Dr. Dan. B. *The Wounded Heart.* NavPress Publishing Group, 1992.

Alsobrook, David. *The Accuser.* Paducah, KY. David Alsobrook Ministries, 1983.

Anderson, Neil T. *The Bondage Breaker.* Eugene, OR. Harvest House Publishers, 1990.

Anderson, Neil. *The Steps to Freedom in Christ.* Gospel Light, 2001.

Arthur, Kay. *Standing Firm in These Last Days.* Eugene, OR. Harvest House Publishers, 2002.

Baars, Conrad, M.D. *Born Only Once.* Franciscan Herald Press, 2001.

Baars, Conrad W., M.D. *Healing the Unaffirmed.* St. Paul's Publishing, 2002.

Bach, George R., and Goldbert, Dr. Herbert. *Creative Aggression.* Wellness Institute, 1974.

Bach, George R. and Wyden, Peter. *The Intimate Enemy.* Avon Books, 1983.

Backus, William. *Finding the Freedom of Self-Control.* Bethany House Publishers, 1988.

Backus, William and Candace. *Untwisting Twisted Relationships.* Bethany House, 1988.

Backus, William, and Chapian, Marie. *Telling Yourself the Truth.* Bethany House, 2000.

Basham, Don and Prince, Derek. *The Unseen War.* New Wine Books, 1982.

Basham, Don. *Deliver Us from Evil.* Chosen Books, 1972.

Beattie, Melody. *Co-Dependent No More.* Hazelden, 1986.

Bennet, Dennis. *How to Pray for the Release of the Holy Spirit.* Bridge-Logos Publishers, 1985.

Bennett, Rita. *How to Pray for Inner Healing for Yourself and Others.* Grand Rapids, MI. Fleming H. Revell Co., 1984.

Bevere, John. *The Bait of Satan.* Charisma House, 2004.

Brown, Rebecca, M.D. *He Came to Set the Captives Free.* Whitaker House, 1992.

Brown, Rebecca, M.D. *Prepare for War.* Check Publications, 1992.

Browning, D.C. *Everyman's Dictionary of Quotations and Proverbs.* J.M. Dent & Sons Ltd.1982

Bussell, Harold. *Unholy Devotion.* Zondervan, 1983.

Copeland, Gloria. *God's Will Is Prosperity.* Kenneth Copeland Publications, 1987.

Campbell, Dr. Ross. *How to Really Love Your Child.* Cook Communication Ministries, 1992.

Campbell, Dr. Ross. *How to Really Love Your Teenager.* Victor Books, 1993.

Carnes, Patrick, *Out of the Shadows, Understanding Sexual Addiction.* Net Library, Inc. 1994

Carothers, Merlin. *Power in Praise.* Bridge-Logos Publishing, 1993.

Carothers, Merlin. *Prison to Praise.* Logos Publishing, 1970.

Carter, Dr. Les. *Imperative People: Those Who Must Control.* Thomas Nelson Publishers, 1991.

Chamber, Oswald, *My Utmost for His Highest.* Dodd, Mead & Company. 1935. Renewed 1963

Chapman, Gary. Hope for the Separated: Wounded Marriages Can Be Healed. Moody Publishers, 2005.

Clark, Jean Illsley and Connie Dawson, Growing *Up Again*, Hazeldon Education. 1989

Christensen, Evelyn. *Battling the Prince of Darkness.* Victor Books, 1990.

Cloud, Dr. Henry, and Townsend, Dr. John. *Boundaries.* Zondervan, 2002.

Cole, Edwin Louis. *Maximized Manhood.* Whitaker House, 1982.

Comiskey, Andrew. *Pursuing Sexual Wholeness.* Charisma House, 1989.

Conn, Charles Paul. *Father Care.* W Publishing Group, 1985.

Conway, Jim and Sally. *Your Marriage Can Survive a Mid-Life Crisis.* Nashville, TN. Thomas Nelson Publishers, 1987.

Cornwall, Judson. *Praying the Scriptures: Communicating with God in His Own Words.* Lake Mary, FL, Creation House, 1990.

Cumbey, Constance. *The Hidden Dangers of the Rainbow.* Huntington House Pub., 1985.

Crabb, Dr. Larry, and Allender, Dr. Dan. *Hope When You're Hurting.* Zondervan Pub. 1997.

Dawson, John. *Taking Our Cities for God—How to Break Spiritual Strongholds.* Lake Mary, FL. Creation House, 1989.

Dawson, John. *Healing America's Wounds.* Regal Books, 1994.

Decker, Ed, and Hunt, Dave. *The God Makers.* Harvest House Publishers, 1997.

Dickason, C. Fred. *Demon Possession & the Christian, A New Perspective.* Moody Press, 1989.

Dispenza, Dr. Joe, *Evolve Your Brain*, 2007.

Dufresne, Ed. *Praying God's Word; A Practical Guide to Victorious Prayer.* Springdale PA, Whitaker House, 1982.

Enroth, Ronald. *Youth, Brainwashing, and the Extremist Cults.* Zondervan, 2000.

Frangipane, Francis. *Discerning of Spirits; Unmasking the Enemies of the Church,* Cedar Rapids, IA. Arrow Publications, 1991.

Frangipane, Francis. *Prevailing Prayer; Becoming a House of Prayer.* Cedar Rapids, IA., Arrow Publications, 1994.

Frangipane, Francis. *The Divine Antidote.* Cedar Rapids, Iowa. Arrow Publications 1994.

Frangipane, Francis. *The Three Battlegrounds.* Advancing Church Publications. 1989

Frangipane, Francis. *This Day We Fight! Breaking the Bondage of a Passive Spirit,* Grand Rapids, MI. Chosen, 2005.

Frank, Jan. *Door of Hope—Recognizing and Resolving the Pains of Your Past.* Nashville, TN. Thomas Nelson Publishers, 1995

Freer, Harold Wiley. *Growing in the Life of Prayer.* Westlake, Ohio. Spiritual Life Clinic, 1972.

Friesen, James D., Ph.D. *More than Survivors.* Resource Publications, 1997.

Friesen, James D., Ph.D. *Uncovering the Mystery of MPD.* Research Publications, 1997.

Garrison, Mary. *The Keys to the Kingdom Are Binding, Loosing and Knowledge.* P.O. Box 384, Villa Rica, Georgia, 1982.

Garrison, Mary. *How to Try a Spirit.* Mary Garrison, 1976.

George, Carl F., Revell, Fleming H. *The Coming Church Revolution; Empowering Leaders for the Future.* 1991.

Goll, Jim D. *The Coming Prophetic Revolution.* Grand Rapids, MI. Chosen Books, 2001.

Green, Michael. *I Believe in Satan's Downfall.* Hodder & Stoughton Religious, 1995.

Hagee, John. *Jerusalem Countdown.* Lake Mary, FL. Frontline, 2006.

Hammond, Frank. *Overcoming Rejection.* Impact Christian Books, Inc., 1987.

Hammond, Frank and Ida Mae. *Pigs in the Parlor.* Impact Christian Books, Inc., 1973.

Hamon, Jane. *The Cyrus Decree.* Santa Rosa Beach, FL. Christian International, 2001.

Hamon, Dr. Bill. *Apostles Prophets and the Coming Moves of God.* Santa Rosa Beach, FL, Christian International, 1997.

Harley, Willard F. *His Needs, Her Needs: Building an Affair-Proof Marriage.* Revell 2001.

Harper, Michael. *Spiritual Warfare.* Bridge-Logos Publishers, 1970.

Hayford, Jack. *Prayer Is Invading the Impossible.* Bridge-Logos Publishing, 1982.

Hayford, Jack. *Rebuilding the Real You.* Regal Books, 1986.

Hegstrom, Paul. *Angry Men and the Women Who Love Them.* Beacon Hill Press, 1999.

Herman, Judith, M.D. *Trauma and Recovery.* Basic Books, 1992.

Hoshor, Lois A. *The Bride Wears Combat Boots.* Mobile, Alabama. Companion Press, 1998.

Hunt, David. *Peace, Prosperity, and the Coming Holocaust.* Harvest House Publishers, 1983.

Hunt, Dave. *The Cult Explosion.* Irvine, CA. Harvest House Publishers, 1980.

Jabay, Earl. *Kingdom of Self.* Plainfield, N.J., Logos International, 1974.

Jackson, John Paul. *Unmasking the Jezebel Spirit.* Streams Publications, 2002.

Jacobs, Cindy. *Possessing the Gates of the Enemy.* Chosen Books, 1994.

Joyner, Rick. *The Surpassing Greatness of His Power.* New Kensington, PA, Whitaker House

Kendall, R. T. *Total Forgiveness.* Charisma House, 2002, 2007.

Kennedy, D. James. *Knowing the Whole Truth.* Fleming G. Revell Co, 1985.

LaHaye, Tim. *Anger Is a Choice.* Zondervan, 2002.

LaHaye, Tim. *Spirit Controlled Temperament.* Tyndale House Publishers, 1993.

LaHaye, Tim. *The Act of Marriage.* Zondervan, 1998.

Larson, Bob. *Larson's Book on Cults.* Tyndale House Publishers, 1989.

Lindsey, Hal. *Satan Is Alive and Well on Planet Earth.* Zondervan, 1972.

Linn, Dennis, and Linn, Matthew. *Healing Life's Hurts.* Paulist Press, 1978.

Littauer, Fred and Florence. *Freeing Your Mind from Memories That Bind.* Nelson Word Publishing Group, 1992.

Lockwood, Craig. *Other Altars.* CompCare Publishers, *1993.*

Gill, A.L. (Compiler). *God's Promises for Your Every Need.* Thomas Nelson Publishers, 1995.

MacGregor, Lorri. *Coping with the Cults.* Delta, B.C., Canada. MacGregor Ministries, 1983.

Malone, Dr. Henry. *Portals to Cleansing—Taking Back Your Land from the Hands of the Enemy* Irving, TX. Vision Life Publications, 2002.

Martin, George. *To Pray As Jesus.* Ann Arbor, Michigan. Servant Books, 1978.

Martin, Walter. *Kingdom of the Cults.* Bethany House Publishers, 1997.

Martin, Walter. *The New Cults.* Vision House Publishers, 1980.

Maudlin, Karen. *Sticks and Stones.* Thomas Nelson Publishers, 2002.

Mayer, Dr. Robert S. *Satan's Children.* Putnam Adult, 1991.

McAll, Dr. Kenneth. *Healing the Family Tree.* London, England. Sheldon Press, 1982.

McDowell, Josh. *Building Your Self-Image.* Tyndale House Publishers, 1973.

McDowell, Josh. *Right from Wrong.* Word Publishing, 1994.

McMillen, S.I., M.D. *None of These Diseases.* David E. Stern, 2000.

McNutt, Francis. *Healing.* Ave Maria Press, 1974.

McNutt, Francis. *The Prayer That Heals.* London, United Kingdom. Hodder & Stoughton, Ltd.,1982.

Means, Pat. *The Mystical Maze.* Campus Crusade for Christ, 1976.

Nee Watchman. *Spiritual Authority.* Christian Fellowship Publishers, 1972.

Osborne, Cecil G. *The Art of Understanding Your Mate.* Zondervan, 1998.

Pakkala, Alaine. *Taking Every Thought Captive: Spiritual Workouts to Help Renew Your Mind in God's Truth.* Lydia Press, 1995.

Parshall, Craig and Janet. *The Light in the City.* Thomas Nelson Publishers, 2000.

Passantino, Robert and Gretchen. *Answers to the Cultist at Your Door.* Harvest House Publishers, 1981.

Payne, Leanne. *Crisis in Masculinity.* Baker Books, 1995.

Payne, Leanne. *Restoring the Christian Soul.* Baker Books, 1996.

Payne, Leanne. *The Healing of the Homosexual.* Baker Books, 1996.

Payne, Leanne. *The Broken Image.* Baker Book House, *196.*

Payne, Leanne. *The Healing Presence.* Baker Books, 1995.

Peizer, Dave. *A Child Called "IT".* Health Communications, Inc., Deerfield Beach, Florida, 1995

Peters, David. *Betrayal of Innocence.* W Publishing Group, 1989.

Pierce, Chuck D. and Sytsema, Rebecca Wagner. *The Future War of the Church.* Regal Books, 2001.

Pierce, Chuck, D. and Sytsema, Rebecca Wagner. *Ridding Your Home of Spiritual Darkness* Wagner Publications, 2000.

Pierce, Chuck, D. and Sytsema, Rebecca Wagner. *Protecting Your Home from Spiritua Darkness.* Ventura, CA. Regal from Gospel Light, 2000.

Powell, John. *The Secret of Staying in Love.* Thomas More Association, 1995.

Powell, John. *Why Am I Afraid to Love?.* Zondervan, 1999.

Powell, John. *Why Am I Afraid to Tell You Who I Am?* Thomas More Association, 1995.

Prince, Derek. *Blessing or Curse, You Can Choose!* Chosen Books, 2006.

Ridenour, Fritz. *So What's the Difference?* Gospel Light Publications, 2001.

Reisman, Dr. Judith A. and Edward W. Eichel. *Kensey, Sex and Fraud.* Huntington House Publishers, 1990

Sanford, Agnes. *The Healing Gifts of the Spirit.* Harper One, 1984.

Sanford, John and Paula. *Healing the Wounded Spirit.* Victory House, 1985.

Sanford, John and Paula. *Restoring the Christian Family.* Logos Publishing, 1980.

Sanford, John and Paula. *The Transformation of the Inner Man.* Victory House Publishers, 1982.

Savard, Liberty. *Shattering Your Strongholds; Freedom from Your Struggles.* Bridge-Logos Publishers, 1993.

Schaeffer, Brenda. *Is It Love or Addiction?* Hazelden PES., 1997.

Seamands, David. *Healing Grace.* Victor Books, 1988.

Seamands, David. *Healing for Damaged Emotions.* Victor Books, 1981.

Seamands, David. *Healing of Memories.* Victor Books, 1985.

Seamands, David. *Putting Away Childish Things.* Victor Books, 1993.

Shackleford, Robert, with Kelly, John. *Familiar Spirits.* Delta Publishing, 1987.

Sheets, Dutch and Pierce, Chuck D. *Releasing the Prophetic Destiny of a Nation.* Shippensburg, PA. Destiny Image Publishers, Inc, 2005.

Sheets, Dutch. *Intercessory Prayer: How God Can Use Your Prayers to Move Heaven* and *Earth.* Ventura, CA. Regal Books, 1996.

Sheets, Dutch. *Praying for America.* Ventura, California. Regal Books, Gospel Light, 2001.

Smalley, Gary. *If Only He Knew: What No Woman Can Resist.* Zondervan Publications, 1997.

Smalley, Gary. *For Better or For Best.* Zondervan Publications, 1996.

Smalley, Gary and Trent, John. *The Blessing.* Thomas Nelson Publishers, 2004.

Smalley, Gary and Trent, John. *The Hidden Value of a Man: The Incredible Impact of A Man on His Family.* Focus on the Family Publishing, 1994.

Smalley, Gary. *The Joy of Committed Love.* Zondervan, 1998.

Smith, Dr. Ed. *Beyond Tolerable Recovery.* Family Care Publishing, Campbellsville, KY, 1999.

Smoke, Jim and Guest, Lisa. *Growing Through Divorce.* Harvest House Pub., 1995.

Solomon, Charles R. *The Ins and Outs of Rejection.* Charles R. Solomon, 1994.

Streeter, Carole Sanderson. *Finding Your Place After Divorce.* Harold Shaw Pub.1992.

Stringfellow, Alan B., Lit. D. *Great Truths of the Bible.* Hensley Publishing, 1980.

Sumrall, Dr. Lester. *Demonology and Deliverance.* Volume 1. Sumrall Publishing, 2001.

Sumrall, Lester. *Overcoming Compulsive Desires.* Strang Communication Company, 1990.

Tapscott, Betty. *Ministering Inner Healing Biblically.* Tapscott Ministries, 1988.

Teykl, Dr.Terry. *Pray the Price.* Prayer Point Press, 1997.

Thurman, Dr. Chris. *Lies We Believe.* Thomas Nelson Publishers Inc. Nashville, TN., 1999

Torrey, R.A. *How to Obtain Fullness of Power.* Murfreesboro, TN. Sword of the Lord Pub.1897

Vredevelt, Pamela, and Rodriguez, Kathryn. *Surviving the Secret.* Fleming H. Revell, Company, 1992.

Wagner, C. Peter. *Freedom from the Religious Spirit.* Ventura, California. Rega Books, 2005.

Wagner, C. Peter. *Seven Power Principles That I Didn't Learn in Seminary.* Wagner Publications, 2000.

Wagner, C. Peter. *Warfare Prayer; How to Seek God's Power and Protection in the Battle to Build His Kingdom.* Ventura, CA. Regal Books, 1992.

Wagner, James K. *Blessed to Be a Blessing; How to Have an Intentional Healing Ministry in Your Church.* Nashville, TN. The Upper Room, 1980.

Walter, Richard. *Forgive and Be Free.* Zondervan, 1983.

Wanderer, Zev. *Letting Go.* Grand Central Publications, 1986.

Warren, Rick. *The Purpose Driven life.* Zondervan, 2002

Wheat, Ed. *Love Life for Every Married Couple.* Zondervan, 1997.

White, Ann. *Healing Adventure.* Sovereign World Ltd., 1989.

Whyte, Maxwell. *Dominion Over Demons.* Springfield, PA. Whitaker House, 1973.

Whyte, Maxwell. *Power of the Blood.* Whitaker House, 1973.

Wright, Norman. *Communication: Key to Your Marriage.* Regal Books, 2000.

HEALING THE HEART

Reference Notes

SESSION ONE: INTRODUCTION

Pg.5— **THE HUMAN BODY**—D.C. Joe Dispenza, Chiropractor, states in *Rewiring Your Brain to a* New Reality ©2013 (1)

Pg.6,7— **DENDRITES/LIMBIC SYSTEM** Caroline Leaf, *Who Switched Off My Brain*, USA, Inc. publisher, *2008 (1)*

Pg.7–9— **STRESS BALL THEORY—BIO-CHEMICAL PATHWAY, CYCLE OF STRESS**—from *Irritable Bowel Syndrome* by Dr. William B. Salt II.) (2)

Pg. 9— **BIO-CHEMICAL PATHWAY/ INHIBITORY PATHWAY,**

Pg. 10— **AMYGDALA**—*Who Switched Off My Brain*, Dr. Caroline Leaf, PhD., author of *Who Switched on Your Brain* USA., Inc., publisher, 2008) (2)

Pg. 11— **THE HEART'S BRAIN**—Gary Schwartz, PhD., University of Arizona, study; Internal Medicine; electroencephalograms (EEG)©—Communication Pathways—brain waves. (1)

Pg. 11— **HEART COMMUNICATIONS**—*Molecules of Emotion* by Dr. Candace Pert, (UK: Simon and Schuster, 1997) (1)

Pg. 11— **THE CRUCIAL LINK**, *Deadly Emotions* by Don Colbert, M.D., (communication with our heart) (1)

Pg. 12— **STATISTICS—Opiate Epidemic Statistics—Center of Science & Disease 2017—Breakdown of Families & Culture,**

Pg. 12— **FUNCTIONS OF THE AMYGDALA**—John Futty, Science Section, The Columbus Dispatch, Oct. 29, 2002—Limbic System (1)

Pg.15— **CHART—SYSTEM DAMAGE DUE TO STRESS AND TRAUMA**—Dr. Caroline Leaf, *Who Switched off My Brain*, USA, Inc., publisher, 2008 (3)

SESSION TWO: THE POWER OF THE MIND

Pg. 16— **FAITH AND FEAR**—quote from Don Colbert, M.D., *Deadly Emotions* (2)

Pg. 19— **CHILDHOOD TRAUMA**—*The Traumatized Child*, ©2004 by Margaret Blanstein (1)

Pg. 19— **CHILDHOOD EXPOSURE TO TRAUMA**—*Getting to the Heart of Healing* by Dr. Bryan Post, ©Post Institute for Family-Centered Therapy (1)

Pg. 19— **DEVELOPMENTAL PROBLEMS**—*Stages of Child Development* © by Dr. Erik Erikson. *Growing Up Again*, Hazelden Education, ©1989 by Jean Illsley-Clarke and Connie Dawson, *Spiritual Warfare for the Wounded*, © 1992, Servant Publications, Dr. Mark Johnston, Author (1)

Reference Notes

Pg. 24-26— **SYSTEMATIC PROCESS FOR RESOLVING UNRESOLVED CONFLICT**—from *Why We Can't "Just Get Over It": Healing the Lasting Effects of Prolonged Stress and Trauma* by Millie McCarty, M.A., LPCC, Copyright 2009. (1)

Pg. 25— **MEMORY AND DISSOCIATION**—J. S. Nemiah, *Early Concepts of Trauma, Memory & Dissociation,* American Psychiatric Press, 1995. (1)

SESSION THREE—DEALING WITH ANGRY PEOPLE

Pg. 28— <u>**DEALING WITH ANGRY PEOPLE**</u>—Andrew Newberg, M.D., *How God Changes the Brain,* Ballantine Books, NY ©2009. (1)

<u>**BOUNDARIES**</u>—Dr. Henry Cloud and Dr. John Townend, Zondervan, ©1992 (1)

Pg. 29-30— <u>**COGNITIVE DISTORTION**</u>S—*Feeling Good* by David D. Burns, M.D., Wholecare, ©1999 (1)

Pg. 31— <u>**THOUGHTS—ROOT OF PAIN—FLASHBACKS AND TRIGGERS**</u>, Dr. Caroline Leaf, M.D., *Who Switched off My Brain?* ©2008 (4)

Pg. 34— **THE CENTRAL NERVOUS SYSTEM—MAIN TARGET OF TOXIC THOUGHTS**

Pg. 34— **IMMUNE SYSTEM, CHEMICAL IMBALANCE**

Pg. 35— <u>**SEVEN FACTORS IN REVERSING THOUGHTS AND BEHAVIORS**</u>—Dr. Joe Dispenza, (3) Rewiring Your Brain to a New Reality

Pg. 36— <u>**REVERSING THE PROCESS**</u>—Research Project at Stanford University by Dr. Fred Luskin, Director of the Stanford Forgiveness Project (1)

Pg. 38— **GETTING TO THE ROOT**—Book: *"A Child Called "It"* by Dave Pelzer (Health Communications, Inc., Deerfield Beach, Fla., ©1995 (1)

Pg. 38— <u>Born Only Once</u>—Intra-Womb Bonding© by Dr. Conrad Barrs, M.D. (2)

Pg. 39— **FROM DARKNESS INTO LIGHT**

Pg. 45— **DIAGRAM: DAN'S CYCLE OF DYSFUNCTION** –Created by Millie McCarty (2004) © created for Pathways to Hope and Healing, ©2003 Ambris Publishing (3)

Pg. 45-47— **Dan's Defense Mechanisms** & System Damage, DAN'S CYCLE OF ILLUMINATION

Pg. 45— **FIVE STEPS OF SHEDDING THE LIGHT**: Cycle of Illumination—Created by Millie McCarty (2003) ©for Pathways to Hope and Healing 2003 Ambris Publishing (4)

SESSION FIVE—FROM DARKNESS TO LIGHT

Pg. 48— **WINDOWS TO THE SOUL**—<u>**JO-HARI WINDOW**</u>—Developed by Joseph Luft and Harry Ingham—1955—*www.communicationskills/johariwindow-model* (1)

Pg. 49— <u>**DEVELOPMENTAL SCARS CHART**</u> from *Growing Up Again* by Jean Illsley Clark and Connie Dawson, Hazelden Education, 1989 (2)

Pg. 50-52— **Generational Sins, Blessings and Curses**

Pg. 53-66— <u>**GENOGRAM**</u>—Best resource: *Genograms in Family Assessment* by Monica McGoldrick & Randy Gerson, Norton Publishing, 1985, (conference notes and handouts). (1)

SESSION SIX—EQUIPPING GOD'S PEOPLE

Pg. 60— *The Coming Church Revolution: Empowering Leaders for the Future,* Carl F. George, Fleming H. Revell, Publisher; Grand Rapids, MI, ©1994 (1)

Pg. 63— **EQUIPPING FOR WARFARE** from Chapter One, *Pathways to Hope and Healing* by Millie McCarty, ©2003 Ambris Publishing. (6)

SESSION SEVEN—WEB OF LIES

Pg. 73-74— *The Lies We Believe* by Dr. Chris Thurman, Thomas Nelson, 2002 (4)

Pg. 74-75— **MEMORIES HOLD LIES**—*Ishbane's Conspiracy* by Randy Alcorn (1)

Pg. 76-79— **DEFENSE MECHANISMS** by Dr. Chris Thurman, Psychologist, Thomas Nelson (2)

Pg. 82-93— **CYCLE OF SIN AND ADDICTION** Adapted from *Out of the Shadows, Understanding Sexual Addiction* by Patrick Carnes, ©1994, Net Library, Inc. (2)

SESSION EIGHT—THE FAMILY SYSTEMS MODEL

Pg. 84— **FAMILY SYSTEMS MODEL**—Best reference: Bowen Family Systems Theory materials. My material came from my workshop notes from a training for Human Growth & Development Training by Foster-Gamble Industry, 1975-76. (1)

Pg. 84— Diagram—**THE FAMILY SYSTEM MODEL**—(Rules, Roles, Rituals, Standards, Beliefs, Values)—the **FORMATION PROCESS** + World Influences (Education, Entertainment, Religion, Government, Economy, Media) Personal Growth & Development Seminar by Proctor and Gamble 1970's by Millie McCarty (1)

Pg. 88 **FAMILY MAKES A DIFFERENCE** (Four Types of Families (Authoritarian, Chaotic, Rigid, Showcase). **FOUR BASIC TYPES OF FAMILIES** (author undocumented) (1)

Pg. 89-90— **FOUR BASIC TYPES OF FAMILIES**—from conference notes 1980's. Best resource: Bowen Family Systems Theory, Peter Titelman, PhD. 1990) (1)

SESSION NINE—BREAKING FREE

Pg. 94— **GUIDE TO SPIRITUAL SURGERY**—*Right from Wrong* by Josh McDowell, Word Publishing, 1994. (1)

Pg. 98— **FORGIVENESS**—*Total Forgiveness* by R. T. Kendall, ©2002, Charisma House (1)

Pg. 115–117— **Bibliography—Recommended Books**
Pg. 119— **PRAYER MINISTRY QUESTIONNAIRE**—(handout) intake form developed for Lighthouse Counseling 1981—revised to include portions of Neil Anderson's material, Harvest House, 1993. (5)

PRAYER MINISTRY QUESTIONNAIRE

Name _____
Address _____
City/State/Zip _____ Phone _____
Age _____ Sex _____ Birthplace _____
Education (highest grade completed) _____
Are you currently employed and/or going to school? If so, where? _____
_____
Is there anything significant about your current or past work or school experience that we should know?
_____
_____

Were you raised by anyone other than your parents? _____
If so, explain. _____
_____

Are you adopted? _____
How many children in your childhood family? _____
Where are you in your family line of siblings? _____
Relationship to father in childhood: Good _____ Bad _____ Indifferent _____
Relationship to mother in childhood: Good _____ Bad _____ Indifferent _____
Relationship to siblings in childhood: Good _____ Bad _____ Indifferent _____
Has there been significant change in any of these relationships? _____
Explain: _____
_____
What of the following did you experience during your childhood?
Broken home _____ Stammering _____ Other learning problems _____ Loneliness _____
Removed from home _____ Bed wetting _____ Nail biting _____ Sexual encounters _____
Sleep walking _____ Incest _____ Excessive fear _____ Physical disabilities _____
Frequent illnesses _____ Night terrors _____ Learning disabilities _____ Serious illnesses _____
Status of Parents:
Good marital relationship   Yes _____ No _____
Alcoholic _____ Drugs _____ Divorced _____ Separated _____ Deceased _____
Other _____
Parents religious background _____
Marital status: Married _____ Separated _____ Divorced _____ Single _____ Widowed _____
If married, for how many years? _____
If married previously, how many times? _____
How many children do you have? _____
What is your current relationship with your children? _____
With whom are you now living? _____

PERSONAL HISTORY QUESTIONNAIRE

Church affiliation: Present _____ Past _____
Born Again _____ Date _____
Water Baptism _____ Date _____
Infant baptism _____ Church _____
How often do your current attend church? _____
Do you have regular devotions in the Bible? _____
Do you find prayer difficult? _____
Do you listen to music regularly? _____ What type do you enjoy most? _____
How many hours of TV do you watch per week?
Are you a veteran of any foreign wars? _____ If so, which one(s)? _____
Is there any part of your life (a large block of time) that you don't remember? _____
Have you done any foreign travel? _____ If so, where? _____
Does your name have any particular significance as to family tradition or cultural or national heritage? _____
Did your parents wish you were of the opposite sex? _____
In your opinion, did your parents wish you had never been born? _____
Have there been any major traumas in your life? _____

Which of the following have you struggled with?

	Past	Now		Past	Now
Daydreaming	___	___	Lustful thoughts	___	___
Headaches	___	___	Thoughts of inadequacy	___	___
Fantasy	___	___	Blasphemous thoughts	___	___
Insecurity	___	___	Obsessive thoughts	___	___
Doubts	___	___	Compulsive thoughts	___	___
Chronic pain	___	___	Dizziness	___	___
PMS	___	___			

Which of the following emotions have you had difficulty controlling?

	Past	Now		Past	Now
Frustration	___	___	Fear of death	___	___
Anger	___	___	Fear of losing your mind	___	___
Loneliness	___	___	Fear of suicide	___	___
Anxiety	___	___	Fear of hurting loved ones	___	___
Bitterness	___	___	Depression	___	___
Hatred	___	___	Worthlessness	___	___

HEALING THE HEART

Trauma...is not just pain and suffering...it is rooted in our perceptions and beliefs about what happened and how it was perceived by self and others. It is through these perceptions and beliefs that our life's actions are based.

"Mother!!!!! I didn't Just wake up one morning and decide to be an addict!!!!"

Don't let your perceptions keep you in Bondage!!

Our Systematic Process of Resolving Unresolved Conflict Eternally provides faith-based processes and proven psychological assessment tools that "get to. the root" of the problem and resolves the mental conflict!

Millie McCarty, M.A., LPCC, Author, Pastor, Trainer, CEO

Millie McCarty, M.A., LPCC-S - 2022

Graduating Cum Laude from Defiance College with a B. A. Degree in Religious Education, Millie went on to receive her M.A. degree in Guidance and Counseling from The Ohio State University in 1981 and became a Licensed Professional Clinical Counselor in 1985. Millie's background as a Director of Education at her church and a Parenting Educator as well as a Personal Growth & Development Trainer added to the richness of her knowledge and ability to meet people where their need was.

Widely known in Ohio as a counselor and teacher, Millie served 20 years as the founder and Executive Director of *Lighthouse Counseling Services from 1981—2001*, when she retired to write and teach. Her groundbreaking work in the areas of early childhood sexual, ritual abuse and dissociative identity disorder, has brought healing and restoration through her strategic, systematic design combining faith principles and proven professional strategies to thousands of adult victims of childhood sexual trauma to citizens of Ohio

After retiring, Millie began a ten-year journey of co-writing a case study entitled *RUTH: Secret of the Silenced voices (A Guide to Working with People with Dissociative Identity Disorders)*. During this period from 2002–2012, as a by-product of the case study, Millie wrote her next book *WHY WE CAN'T "Just Get Over It": Healing the Effects of Prolonged Stress and Trauma.* At the same time, developing her *"Systematic Process"* of resolving unresolved conflicts needed for restoration. Millie began being asked to train people from other nations such as: China, Ethiopia, Jamaica, Finland, Haiti, Rwanda and Uganda. Today she is being called to train church leaders at home and abroad in her Systematic Process to equip the church for the great harvest that lies before us.

Systematic Process for Resolving Unresolved Conflict Eternally (SPRUCE)

From 2012–2017 Millie implemented a systematic approach to equipping others with the tools to provide care for survivors of abuse and trauma using her curriculum and implementing other coursework to provide the necessary skills to restore the life skills missed during the time of abuse and trauma. These classes were established as a certification program based on her 35 years of counseling and training. Her goal is to get the curriculum accredited and published to provide this **S**ystematic **P**rocess of **R**esolving **U**nresolved **C**onflict **E**ternally (**SPRUCE**) to all nations.

www.ingramcontent.com/pod-product-compliance
Lightning Source LLC
Chambersburg PA
CBHW081401070526
44583CB00020B/2626